What others say about "How to REALLY use LinkedIn"

"Finally someone explaining why LinkedIn is useful. As a typical Gen X'er, I was starting to get frustrated to hear more and more people talking about the advantages and the fun of being Linked In. Once I got it, I immediately made a profile and started connecting. And if I can do it, so can anybody else!"

Hubert Vanhoe, Vice President, USG People Belgium, www.usgpeople.com

"Put simply, "How to REALLY use LinkedIn" is a must read for anybody who wants to grow their business through networking. Even if you're already a member of a referral or network organization, Jan Vermeiren offers powerfully advanced strategies on how LinkedIn can help you get even more out of your membership!"

Ivan Misner, NY Times Bestselling author and Founder of BNI, www.bni.com

"I have been using LinkedIn for a while now, but other than connecting to people I personally know, I did not use it. This book really gives you structured insights and "off the shelf" tips to increase the effectiveness and the power of your network, and a big help in reaching your goals easier and quicker. Thanks for sharing your expertise, Jan. Strong recommendation to all the people that want to start using their network more efficiently!"

Frank Opsomer, Sales Manager Partner Sales Organization BeLux, Sun Microsystems, www.sun.com

"It is great to read a book that is this practical and gives examples to help you reach your networking goal. Thanks Jan!"

Mary Roll, Career Services Manager International MBA Program, Vlerick Leuven Gent Management School, www.vlerick.com

"This enlightening look at a new form of social media and next-generation communi–cation provides meaningful ideas in an easy-to-read format. Perfect for any age!"

Dr. Nido Qubein, President, High Point University and Chairman, Great Harvest Bread Co., www.nidoqubein.com

"This is an informative and well structured book that everyone who understands the value of networking and building the right connections should read. This book is a must and should be at the top of anyone's reading list this year!"

Paul Bridle, Leadership Methodologist, www.paulbridle.com

"For a marketer networking is a major part building block to do a job. With new social networks coming along it is imperative that these skills are used wisely. This book has helped to sharpen my Linked-in social networking skills and helped focused how to profile myself better to get most out of my network!"

Mic Adam, Director - Executive Center of Innovation, Unisys, www.unisys.com

"Jan Vermeiren has done it! He has written a LinkedIn guide in easy-to-understand language that is a godsend for neophytes and a boon for veteran users as well. Readers internationally will polish their online presence to build more internal and external credibility and learn how to turn connections into more sales and career success!"

Lillian D. Bjorseth, author Breakthrough Networking: Building Relationships That Last, www.duoforce.com

"If there is just one book you buy this year, it should be this one. Social networking is the new marketing medium and LinkedIn is at the forefront. Jan shares all the secrets and strategies in a concise and simple manner and he is undoubtedly the master of LinkedIn. It doesn't matter what business you are in, this book has all the tools to enable you to make more connections and increase productivity!"

Frank Furness, Bestselling Author and International Speaker, www.frankfurness.com

"I thought I knew lots about LinkedIn but "How to REALLY use LinkedIn" goes into every function and process in a simple step-by-step process. Jan, being someone who is also an expert on 'live' networking you of all people have been able to link the online and offline networking systems and principles to ensure this book will be highly prized by people who wish to become modern day all around networkers!"

Will Kintish, UK authority on business networking skills, www.kintish.co.uk

"If you're like me, getting your head around an advanced networking tool like LinkedIn can be quite daunting. Jan Vermeiren has simplified it all - not only by spelling out in easy steps how LinkedIn works as an effective tool to create the right contacts and clients for your business, he also provides priceless wisdom on the fundamentals of intelligent networking. The little time it takes you to read this informative book will save you literally hours online - and impact your business quickly and positively!"

Paul du Toit, Certified Speaking Professional, MD of the Congruence Group, South Africa, www.pauldutoit.net

"If there is one secret that creates business success it would be "networking." Jan Vermeiren's new book "How to REALLY use LinkedIn" is a powerful tool that helps you implement the age old concept of building relationships and maximizing it with 21st Century tools!"

Don Boyer, Creator of The Power of Mentorship book series, www.DonBoyerAuthor.com

"LinkedIn for me was just another website to connect to people. Since I didn't find any added value, I only logged onto the website after somebody sent me an invitation request. However, while reading the book "How to REALLY use LinkedIn", the ideas just kept coming. I had no idea LinkedIn had so much potential. LinkedIn turned from a '13 in a dozen' website into one big opportunity! If you want to create your own network but you have no idea where to start or you haven't got a lot of time ... start by reading this book! It's easy to understand, very practical and full of tips and tricks. See you on LinkedIn!"

Ellen Van Bossuyt, Jr Academy Manager, Euphony Benelux, www.euphony.com

"As a LinkedIn user with over 600 connections and an active blogger since 2004, I can tell when a book has real value. This book has it in spades! You will find more good, quick, easy answers in this book than any of its kind. I've read the others and learned from them, but this one was written by someone like me: a professional speaker and author, a subject expert whose main product is himself and the talent he offers. Every page is easy to read and apply. Buy this book and keep it on your desktop until your thousands of high-value connections cover it up with money!"

Jim Cathcart, author of Relationship Intelligence®: Who's Glad To Know You? http://cathcart.com

"I have been a regular user of LinkedIn for a while so I thought I couldn't learn much more. However I was surprised about the extra dimension "How to REALLY use LinkedIn" gives to this website, especially how to craft a good Profile. Suddenly it makes more sense not only to use LinkedIn more, but also in a way to get better results in less time and in a way that respects all involved parties!"

Christoph Van Doninck, Sales & Marketing Coördinator DPC, Dupont De Nemours, www.dupont.com

"Networks make sure the labor market runs smoothly. Lots of job openings are filled via informal ways. Due to the structural lack of personnel, employers don't have any other choice than look for alternative recruitment channels. When looking for a job or when looking for talented people social networks like LinkedIn can really make the difference. Read "How to REALLY use LinkedIn" and increase your chances on the market!"

Fons Leroy, Managing Director, Vlaamse Dienst voor Arbeidsbemiddeling en Beroepsopleiding (VDAB), www.vdab.be

"The time when it was enough for entrepreneurs to make decent products or render good services is behind us. Running a business is not done on an island anymore. Craftsmanship, a professional drive and creativity remain the core, but communication, PR and selling your product or service are increasingly important. Building a good network is a necessity for every entrepreneur. LinkedIn is one of the tools to do this. "How to REALLY use LinkedIn" explains in a simple, step-by-step approach how to get the maximum out of it!"

Karel Van Eetvelt, Managing Director, Unizo, www.unizo.be

"For several years now, Jan has continued to build a solid reputation as a credible authority in the area of networking. Personally, I have derived many benefits from reading his previous book "Let's Connect", and attending his training courses. In this new book, Jan revisits some tried-and-tested principles about networking, and adds actionable strategies for putting them into practice. For those that are serious about networking, and want to unlock the potential value that LinkedIn holds for them, this book is a definite recommendation!"

Ago Cluytens, Global Head of Marketing, ING Private Banking, www.ing.com

"In the past years LinkedIn has become a fantastic networking tool for entrepreneurs and managers. Unfortunately only few people realize the power of this website, mostly because we lack the knowledge. That's why I'm so glad that Jan took the initiative to write a book about LinkedIn. As a networking expert he is in the best position to share insights and practical tips. Thanks to "How to REALLY use LinkedIn" we can turn LinkedIn into a powerful tool when looking for new business relations or when building our network!"

Peter Desmyttere, Marketing Consultant for Entrepreneurs, www.peterdesmyttere.com

"I thought I knew all there is to know about using LinkedIn. But after reading Jan Vermeiren latest book I've been able to connect faster to higher level profiles and create more value out of my LinkedIn network then ever before. I highly recommend you read this book and implement what you learn!"

Byron Soulopoulos, CEO, Brian Tracy Benelux, www.briantracy.be

"After reading "How to REALLY use LinkedIn," I'm able to better manage my list of professional business contacts. I can also more easily find potential business and have better contact with experienced professionals worldwide. I met Jan for the first time during a sponsorship seminar and since then I read a lot of his interesting online networking publications because this type of networking will be more and more important in the future. It opens a lot of doors for my professional daily communication work!"

Philiep Caryn, International Communication & Sponsorship Quick-Step, www.qsi-cycling.com

"Native English speakers will be aware of the saying, 'Cometh the hour, cometh the man'. In the case of this book we could correctly say, 'Cometh the technology, cometh the book'. Jan Vermeiren's latest book, 'How to REALLY use LinkedIn' is an essential reference work for any business person seriously interested in the power of social networking technology. It's far more useful than an operating manual. Here you'll find excellent strategies for how to get the best from this technology and what's available through the different levels of membership, for example. There is no doubt in my mind that LinkedIn itself has developed tremendously in recent times and this book is being published at just the right time to help people maximize their use of the technology!"

Chris Davidson, Managing Editor, www.ProfessionalSpeakersJournal.com

"How to really use LinkedIn" from Jan Vermeiren really opened my eyes to the possibilities within LinkedIn and how to go about using it in a very efficient and effective way. I am a member of LinkedIn, and don't tend to spend a lot of time on it. This book, however, changed my mind of the possibilities and opportunities and I will start to spend more time on it with Jan, his book as my guide!"

Menno Siebinga, Entrepreneur, martial artist, organizer of the Body& Brein Festival (The Netherlands) and founder of the Siebinga method, www.teamsiebinga.com

"As a network coach and trainer I meet many people that are on LinkedIn, but use it in a rather passive way. Jan's book, "How to REALLY use LinkedIn" makes it very clear what a powerful tool LinkedIn is and it makes you want to start using it right away!"

Daphne Medik, networking coach and trainer, DMM Communication, www.dmcommunication.nl

"This book is a must read for anyone wanting to enhance their networking skills and leverage online networking tools, especially LinkedIn. Jan has provided a practical, comprehensive resource with a large number of strategies to apply daily. As an international productivity expert I am often looking for valuable resources to recommend to my clients to boost their personal and professional productivity – I can highly recommend this book. Based on the foundation of the Golden Triangle of Networking, Jan emphasizes a need to give, ask and thank. Do yourself a favor, invest your time and energy in reading and applying the principles in this book – you will be glad you did!"

Neen James, International Productivity Expert, www.neenjames.com

"Thank you Jan for sharing your knowledge and insights on networking again. I have been on LinkedIn for a while, always realizing that I did not really USE it to its full potential. Now I know why and I know how to change that. "How to REALLY use LinkedIn" gives me the insight and the method to do better. And ... especially, it stimulates me to really act upon the eye openers provided, because the rewards are clearly specified and relevant. Powerful and empowering!"

Katharina Müllen, Transition Manager & Vitality Mentor, WinVitality www.winvitality.eu

"I find myself asked by more and more people how to use LinkedIn effectively. People are becoming more aware of its power and importance, to both individuals and to businesses. Jan has yet again succeeded in providing a clear, concise and hugely readable guide. "How to REALLY use LinkedIn" will move people from beginners to advanced LinkedIn networkers. Read the book, follow the steps and watch the benefits flow your way!"

Andy Lopata, Business Networking Strategist and co-author of '...and Death Came Third! The Definitive Guide to Networking and Speaking in Public, www.lopata.co.uk

"Jan did it again! Once more he shows he is thé networking expert. Not only face-to-face, but also on LinkedIn!"

*Eric Eraly, author of "The Easy To Quit Smoking Method",
www.EnjoyQuitSmoking.com*

"While some of the technology described in this book may change, the networking and communication principles are key to having a successful LinkedIn experience. Live the "givers gain principle" and LinkedIn might be the best business tool you use!"

Jason Alba, CEO of JibberJobber.com and author of I'm on LinkedIn – Now What???, www.jibberjobber.com

"LinkedIn was the first online network I joined back in 2004 and today it's still one of the largest global networks. In the past years lots of extra features and tools were added to the platform and it was about time that someone wrote a comprehensive manual on the use of this brilliant website. Congratulations Jan, "How to REALLY use LinkedIn" does exactly what it says on the label, it's the best and most complete manual on LinkedIn ... This is what we were waiting for !"

Geert Conard, Management Consultant and author of "A Girlfriend in Every City," www.geertconard.com

"We live in a world in which technology is impacting everything that we do, especially the way we build relationships. While face-to-face interaction is important, Jan shows us how LinkedIn is changing the game and is a must for any professional who wants to stay connected and get ahead in their careers!"

Jason Jacobsohn, Chicago networking personality, www.NetworkingInsight.com

"I have read many books about networking and most seem to rehash the same old things. Jan, however, "pushes the envelope" in this book by looking at one of the most underutilized tools that all effective networkers have today: LinkedIn. As the relationship networking revolution continues to capture the attention of everyone worldwide, online networking systems like LinkedIn continue to move to the forefront, and Jan outlines some really useful strategies here on how we can take advantage of this powerful utility. This is a definite must-have!"

Adam J. Kovitz, CEO, Founder & Publisher, The National Networker,
http://thenationalnetworker.com

"Jan shares his secrets behind successfully tapping into the power of your network on LinkedIn. It's amazing how powerful this tool can be if you use it in the right way!"

Scott Bradley, Social Media Specialist, www.NetworkingEffectively.com

"A really useful set of strategies to build your network - one step at a time, one person at a time. Using 3 steps of know, like and trust; Jan Vermeiren demonstrates how to work on building a really useful and diverse network. Nowadays networking is a dynamic mix of offline and online, where 3 questions are still useful to me: "Who are you?", "How are you?" and "How may I help you?" The difference with online networking is the directness and speed with which I can reach huge numbers of people. Networking only calls for a little of my work time and a consistent effort to make it really effective. Set your goals and use the straightforward strategies in "How to REALLY use LinkedIn" for your network!"

Nathaniel Stott, Life Architect, www.lifearchitect.eu

"As a how-to guide, this book contains everything you may need to know about LinkedIn. I've personally found it very useful indeed!"

Mike Southon, Financial Times columnist and co-author of 'The Beermat Entrepreneur," www.beermat.biz

"The good thing about "How to REALLY use LinkedIn" is that it provides excellent insights in the fundamentals, then describes a basic strategy for everybody and then an advanced strategy for several profiles. This makes it worthwhile for every professional!"

Bill Cates, Author of "Get More Referrals Now!", www.referralcoach.com

"Although being a professional speaker on networking for years, it still took me three years to really understand the real powers of LinkedIn. Never before in history of mankind, it was possible to discover the second and the third layer of your network. LinkedIn already rocks when you only want to use it for business opportunities, but the real magic lies in interconnecting the right people and networks that are trying to solve major challenges that we face as human beings, by enabling us to spend our social capital in a much smarter way. To understand why, please read this book!"

Martijn Aslander, Lifehacker - Connector - Resourcerer & public speaker at events, www.martijnaslander.nl

"If you want to find the best people and cultivate profitable relationships by maximizing the world's most powerful social networking tool, then read Jan Vermeiren's outstanding new book, " How to REALLY Use LinkedIn"!

Don Gabor, author of Turn Small Talk Into Big Deals: Using 4 Key Conversation Styles To Customize Your Networking Approach, Build Relationships and Win More Clients, www.dongabor.com

With "How to REALLY use LinkedIn" Jan Vermeiren has written an excellent book for beginners and average users of LinkedIn. It contains practical examples of what you could use LinkedIn for (recruitment, sales, finding suppliers,...), but also links online and offline networking. The reader realizes that the gap between them is in fact not so big at all. This book is a must-read for anyone who wants to know more about what he can accomplish with LinkedIn!"

An De Jonghe, author of Social Networks Around The World: How is Web 2.0 Changing Your Daily Life?", http://andejonghe.blogspot.com

"How to REALLY use LinkedIn" is stimulating, enjoyable and informative. Jan excels at sharing valuable, pragmatic knowledge in this book. I found it to be very helpful, even for seasoned networkers or experienced LinkedIn users, like myself. I recommend this book to better understand the sound principles of networking and to learn more about the amazing power of LinkedIn. It truly is the best LinkedIn book on the planet!"

Bert Verdonck, Lifehacker & Life Coach, http://blog.bertverdonck.com

"Many of my customers tell me they find LinkedIn confusing, complex and time-consuming. Thank goodness Jan has written this book, because I can let my clients have it safe in the knowledge that by reading it they will realize that LinkedIn is a highly effective tool for their business. Plus, they will see that LinkedIn is straightforward, easy to get on with and, when used well, time-efficient. Thankfully Jan's book guides people through the use of LinkedIn in such a friendly way they will be able to use it to truly enhance their business networking for great effect – and quickly. I have absolutely no doubt in recommending this book to my customers – indeed to anyone who uses LinkedIn!"

Graham Jones, Internet Psychologist, www.grahamjones.co.uk

"I love hands-on and practical books. This is one of those rare gems one can put next to one's keyboard as a how-to manual and get (a lot of) things done straightaway. By providing clear insights and a simple, but super effective strategy, Jan Vermeiren shows how everybody can tap into the power of online business networking and more specifically LinkedIn!"

Guido Thys, Corporate Midwife, www.guidothys.nl

"Are you willing to think differently? Are you willing to challenge the current orthodoxy about the use of internet? Jan Vermeiren gives us the right insights for the opportunity to extend our professional network and exchange experiences with professionals in other industries!"

Henno Vos, Managing Director, Flevum Forum Network, www.flevum.nl

"It was to be expected that Jan, as the networking expert in Belgium, would one day write a book on social networks. "How to REALLY use LinkedIn" is a must for all professionals wishing to enter the next era of networking: it contains fascinating insights on the meaningful use of LinkedIn in a business environment; it familiarizes you with the many unknown, interesting features of LinkedIn; and it deals with burning questions around this social network. In short, this book is an indispensable guide to discovering the power of LinkedIn!"

Erik Van den Branden, Director of HR Shared Services, Deloitte Belgium, www.deloitte.com

"Online business networking is a very hot topic. However, many people don't know how to really deal with websites like LinkedIn. "How to REALLY use LinkedIn" gives more than an answer. Highly recommended! "

Astrid De Lathauwer, Chief Human Resources Officer, Belgacom, www.belgacom.com

"I found the big hype around social networking frustrating and confusing until I read How to REALLY use LinkedIn. Thank you, Jan, finally a resource that shows me how to get the best out of social networking while giving my best to all my contacts!"

Garth Roberts, CSP, www.garthroberts.com

"The information in "How to REALLY use LinkedIn" is a powerhouse book of tips, tactics and approaches for raising your personal profile that simply work. LinkedIn is the buzzword in business networking these days and this book shows how to REALLY use it!"

Dr. Tony Alessandra, author of The Platinum Rule and The NEW Art of Managing People, www.alessandra.com

"Great things come from simple and pragmatic methods and that is what Jan Vermeiren succeeded with his latest book. "How to REALLY use LinkedIn" will not only give you clear strategies to increase your network efficiency with the use of LinkedIn, but it will also tell you the real sense and purpose of networking. A must for every professional!"

Vincent De Waele, Business Transformation Director, Mobistar, www.mobistar.be

"This book is an eye-opener – once you've read it you'll see how easy business (or job searching) becomes. By providing clear insights and a simple, but super effective strategy Jan Vermeiren shows how everybody can tap into the power of online business networking and more specifically LinkedIn. "How to REALLY use LinkedIn" is a must-read!"

Jill Lublin, International Speaker and Best Selling Author of Get Noticed...Get Referrals, Guerrilla Publicity, and Networking Magic, www.jilllublin.com

"If you take networking seriously, use LinkedIn. If you take LinkedIn seriously, read this book!"

Edgar Valdmanis, GoldClub Networker/Business Network International (BNI), www.bni.com

How to REALLY use LinkedIn

How to REALLY use LinkedIn

Discover the true power of LinkedIn and how to leverage it for your business and career.

To my network, which was, is and ever will be the catalyst of my inspiration, success and happiness.

"How to REALLY use LinkedIn"

Jan Vermeiren

Published by Booksurge: www.booksurge.com

ISBN: 9781439229637

NUR: 800, 802, 809

Copyright © 2009 by Jan Vermeiren.

Networking Coach: www.networking-coach.com

Website of the book: www.how-to-really-use-linkedin.com

Lay-out and print: Pages, Ghent, Belgium

Cover: Graffito, Ghent, Belgium

Library of Congress Control Number: 2009901615

Table of Contents

Hot Discussion
Topics and Burning Questions

Little known, but interesting features and behavior of LinkedIn

Prologue

LinkedIn and other social and business networking websites have found their place in our society. In the past few years we have seen an explosive and exponential growth of many networks. In the beginning most people were very skeptical about them, but now they are not only here to stay, but they offer opportunities we never had before.

In my job as speaker, trainer and coach about networking and referrals I have seen the value of these networks from the moment they had their tipping point in 2003. As an entrepreneur who is continuously looking for customers, suppliers, employees, partners, media contacts, expert's opinions and other help I personally also have experienced the tremendous power they have.

The past years my team at Networking Coach (www.networking-coach.com) received an ever-increasing stream of questions from participants to our training courses or members from the audience in our presentations about what the value is of online business networks and how to deal with them. And in particular LinkedIn. Many people expressed their resistance and were skeptical about this new way of interacting, but like many other things in life it was more "fear of the unknown." Once I explained and showed how they too could benefit from it and how they could immediately start using it, some of them became the heaviest users of LinkedIn.

Since we got so many questions I was already thinking about writing a book. Not only for the participants of our training courses and presentations, but also to give people who are not able to attend our sessions this valuable information which could take their business or career to the next level(s).

So I was already thinking about writing a book about LinkedIn for a while, but what really triggered me to actually write it, was the moment LinkedIn introduced the "Discussions" functionality in the Groups.

Why was that the trigger? There are many, many online networks these days (you find some more in the back of the book) with different functionality. My biggest "problem" with LinkedIn was that there were no forums or clubs where people could discuss topics, help other people and be helped by other people. If people wanted that functionality they had to be a member of other networking websites or Yahoo or Google Groups (or other forums). But on the other hand LinkedIn was and is by far the largest biggest business networking website (over 34 million users and growing) meaning that if someone already heard of online business networking LinkedIn is the website they mention.

So the moment LinkedIn introduced "Discussions" the obstacle of having to use extra Yahoo or Google Groups fell away. Next to that, thousands of new members with a variety of profiles from all industries keep registering on the website every day making LinkedIn even more interesting for EVERY professional.

Why would an increasing numbers of members make it more interesting to become a member yourself? Think about telephones: they only became interesting when there were enough people to use them. The same applies to LinkedIn.

Before I explain the power of networking and how to use LinkedIn as a tool with tremendous leveraging capacity to support you I want to make a few disclaimers:

- The disadvantage of writing a book about things that happen on the web is that some functionality might be different than as described. Some things might have changed or even deleted and definitely more functionality will have been added. For example, when I took a week off to write the first version of this book (November 2008) LinkedIn added the Applications and introduced a new search function. These changes are also the reason I will avoid using screenshots. But I want you to get as much out of your LinkedIn membership as possible so to get a free LinkedIn Profile Assessment and to be up-to-date of new functionality and new strategies, you can register for free at www.how-to-really-use-linkedin.com/updates.html.

- Although I will go into the details of LinkedIn, I won't discuss all basic functionality. If you really need lots of screenshots and basic explanations about the functions of LinkedIn, there are other books to help you with that like "How to Succeed in Business using LinkedIn" by Eric Butow and Kathleen Taylor or "LinkedIn for Dummies" by Joel Elad.

- I don't have any business relationship or business interest in LinkedIn. My company Networking Coach and I are independent from LinkedIn and any other website.

- Although I might be able to answer all your questions about LinkedIn, there is a good Customer Service at LinkedIn. They not only have FAQ pages where you can find almost all answers to questions (these are also the pages I turn to when I have a question), but they also they have a help desk with real people who respond to questions (unbelievable for help desks these days, isn't it ☺). You will find the "Help" function on top of each page. Or you can go to:
http://linkedin.custhelp.com

So what is this book about then? It gives you insights in what networking is about and how to use the fantastic tool LinkedIn is to tap into the power of your network to reach any of your professional goals whatever function you might have and whatever industry you are in. This book starts from a practical point of view: your current job and how you can improve doing your job (better results in less time) by tapping into the power of your network using LinkedIn.

Enjoy !

Jan

PS: This book only has value when you apply the information, tips and wisdom you receive. My advice: read this book once to understand the ideas and strategies. Then read it again and start applying tip after tip. Don't apply them all at once, because you might feel overwhelmed. Pick three ideas that you can start using immediately and when you have integrated them in your life then pick the next ones.

PPS: To help you get even more value out of this book we have started the "Global Networking Group" on LinkedIn (http://www.linkedin.com/groups?home=&gid=1393777).
It is open to anyone who wants to play by the rules of this Group.
So come and join us!

What Is (the value of) Networking?

Two of the remarks we hear the most in our training courses or presentations are:

1. "Why do I have to network? What is in it for me?"

2. Especially when it comes down to online networking: "Those people with thousands of connections, are they not just name collectors? I don't want to be like them."

What we have experienced is that it is important to understand the value and fundamentals of networking before diving into what LinkedIn can do for us and how to use it.

In my book, "Let's Connect!" I already explained in detail which dynamics form the foundation of networking and of any networking strategy. In this chapter I will explain some of them again (without going too much into details) so you understand why and what we do in the next chapters. Please read this chapter very attentively because understanding and applying these fundamental principles will make a huge difference in using LinkedIn.

First let's look at some benefits networking can have and then go deeper in some fundamental principles of networking online and off-line.

What are the benefits of networking?

Many people have already heard other people say: networking is important. And then the person for instance explains how it helps in sales. But if you are not responsible for any sales results you probably won't listen.

So here is a list of 26 reasons why networking is important. These reasons are the main ones we got from the thousands of participants of our networking and referral training courses and presentations. I published this list on my blog (www.janvermeiren.com) on March 1, 2008, but it is still relevant.

Sales related

1) Maintaining relationship with current customers

2) Meeting new prospects

3) Getting referrals to new prequalified prospects

4) Receiving referrals to other departments at current customers

5) Word of mouth publicity

6) Creating ambassadors who will tell about you and connect you with the right prospects

Not sales related

7) Finding a new job

8) Finding a new employee or colleague

9) Getting to know the right people who can help you with your career

10) Attracting the right organizations to form partnerships with

11) Notifications when there are important changes (for example when legislation changes)

12) Up-to-date information for work-related topics

13) Knowing about new trends

14) Receiving more visibility as a person or an organization

15) Attracting more opportunities

16) Getting new ideas, new insights and new wisdom

17) Getting another perspective

18) Door openings to people you won't be able to reach on your own

19) Enrichment in every possible way

20) Doing things with more fun

21) Developing as a person

22) Developing as an organization

23) Attracting the right mentors

24) Having a filter (= people from your network) for the massive amounts of information on the Internet and elsewhere

25) Receiving more invitations to (the right) events as a participant, speaker or co-host

26) Security net when something happens

>   26 a - When you are without a job
>
>   26 b - When you have too much work
>
>   26 c - On a personal level (getting the kids out of school, help when renovating your house, babysitter, …)

The rest of this book will show you how LinkedIn can help you to have all these benefits (yes even the babysitter ☺). But let's first look at the foundation of networking: the 2 biggest problems, the 5 fundamental principles and the challenge we all have.

The 2 biggest problems when (online) networking

If people have already given some thought to networking, many times they start going to events, make a profile on a website and start connecting with people.

Then there comes a moment most of them say something like: "I have put some time and effort in it, but I don't have the feeling I get much out of it."

The reason is that they have never thought about:

1.   What their goal is.

2.   Who the people are who are in the best position to help them to reach that goal.

These are the 2 biggest reasons why networking seems to not "pay off" for many people.

But when you reverse it and set your goals and ask yourself the question who might the people who are in the best position to help you reach them, it becomes so much easier. It becomes clear which organizations, online networks and which Groups on those online networks to join. It becomes clear who to reach out to and whom to ask for help and support.

How you approach them and how you will be perceived will make or break your networking efforts. Understanding and applying the 5 fundamental principles of networking will make sure you really get results. So let's look at what they are.

Fundamental Principle 1: Networking Attitude

In my networking book "Let's Connect!" I define the networking attitude as:

> **"Sharing information in a reactive and proactive way without expecting anything immediately in return."**

Let's have a more detailed look at this definition:

- **Information**: in this definition "information" refers to both very general and very specific knowledge. For example, how to record a television program with a video recorder. Or the specific code of the newest software programming language. "Information" is also about business issues, like sales leads, and about simple day-to-day stuff (like "what are the opening hours of the supermarket"). In a professional environment "information" is, for example, a job opening, a sales lead, a new supplier or employee, opportunities for partnerships, interesting training courses or tips to work more efficiently.

- **Sharing**: this involves two parties. Networking is not a one-way street, but a two-or more way boulevard. It is always about a win-win situation, in which all parties are satisfied. What's important in this concept is that you are comfortable with both giving help and making requests.

- **In a reactive and pro-active way**: in the first place this means that you offer information or help when you are asked to do so (reactive). But it goes further than that. You can send people information and connect them to each other, without them asking to do this (pro-active). But, of course, make sure you don't SPAM them. A good approach could be to let them know you have this information and that you are willing to share it. Especially when you don't know people well, this might be a non-confrontational approach.

- **Without expecting anything immediately in return**: in this era of short-term benefits it's not a concept that's immediately embraced by everybody. Let me also stress it is NOT about giving your own products or services away. It is about everything else: what is your attitude when dealing with people. Though it might be hard for some people, this is the one attitude that works best in the long run. This builds trust and makes you more "attractive" to other people.

By giving without expecting anything immediately in return, you will eventually receive much more than your initial "investment." But you never know from whom or when. And that's something many people have difficulties with. In our training courses this is always the start of a lively discussion because only a few people see how they can realize this without investing lots of time and money. We'll see later in this book how we can deal with that and how LinkedIn can help us.

Remember that networking is a **long-term** game that **always involves 2 or more players**. You reap what you've sown. So start sowing (sharing) so you can reap more and faster!

Not knowing and applying the networking attitude is reason number one why people feel that LinkedIn doesn't work for them. Because they are only focused on themselves they don't receive help from other people and get frustrated with the lack of positive responses.

Fundamental Principle 2: The Golden Triangle of Networking

When I talk about the Golden Triangle of Networking many people look at me like I am talking about something mysterious. In fact, it is not mysterious at all, but an easy and effective way to build relationships.

Let's look at the three angles of the Golden Triangle:

Give or Share

This relates back to the networking attitude. What can we give or share with other people. By giving and sharing we improve our relationships with other people.

For many people this is a hard concept because they think in terms of need instead of abundance. They also think if they give something away they don't have it themselves anymore. Though that might be true for physical objects, we live more and more in a knowledge society (especially in the western world). When you share information or knowledge (like I'm doing with you now) you don't lose it. We both have it.

In Let's Connect there are many examples of what we can share with each other. Later in this book we will see how easy LinkedIn makes it for us to share with other people without spending much time.

Ask

When networking it is important to ask other people for their help. This is where the power of the network resides: getting help from other people.

However, many people have difficulties asking for help. In "Let's Connect!" I quote networking expert Donna Fisher from her book "People Power" about the mental barriers many people impose on themselves and the 7 types of conditioning that can influence your networking effectiveness without you even realizing it. These are the reasons why we often don't ask for help and spend too much time figuring things out ourselves.

In my presentations I often ask: "Do you remember the last time someone asked you for some information or for your help and you were able to assist this person? What feeling did you get?" The answer is then: a good, positive and nice feeling.

Then I tell them: "The next time you have a question or need help, but for any reason, any type of conditioning or any mental barrier, you don't ask the question and do it alone, then you prevent other people of having this good, positive and nice feeling."

For many people this helps to see it from a different perspective. For some it is almost a paradigm shift.

While it might be obvious that we improve OUR relationships when giving and sharing with other people, asking is also important to give other people the opportunity to improve THEIR relationship with us.

However, we all had negative experiences in the past when asking questions. Some people didn't respond very well to our questions. That might also have caused us from asking questions and asking for help.

There are two main reasons why this happened in the past:

1. We didn't ask a good question
2. We didn't ask the question in a way that would have given us the best result

Let's look at this in more detail.

What does a good question look like?

A good question is like a good goal: it has to be as specific as possible. The more specific, the better. Compare it with a search engine like Google. When you enter the word "networking" you get 296,000,000 hits. Let's assume you are looking for a networking coach. You begin to scroll down and look at the results. After half an hour you are tired and frustrated because you didn't find what you were looking for. But if you start a new search with the exact phrase "networking coach" you only get 24,000 results. The odds that you find what you are looking for have increased substantially! Do the same with your requests: make them more specific.

Another example: someone I knew lost his job and asked me: "You have lots of contacts, can you help me to get a new job?" Probably I could have got him on the way, but where on earth should I have started? This question was so vague that in fact I was not able to help him.

So what did I do? I asked questions: what experience do you have, which languages do you speak, what are your goals, what is your added value to an organization, what are your expectations and in which region do you want to work? And finally we got to the point where I could help him. It became clear that he had 6 years experience in IT, more specifically programming in Visual Basic, C++ and .Net, was trilingual (Dutch, French, English) and was looking for a company in the vicinity of Antwerp, Belgium. This narrowed the search in my brain and in my database. And I was able to introduce him to two potential employers.

> **Networking success tip**: help others to help you. Be specific!

If you want a good answer: ask a good question. Prepare yourself. Think about what you want and how other people can contribute to reaching your goal. That way you give the signal that you made some effort yourself to get the best possible answer. People appreciate this. And they don't always appreciate you using their time to "prepare yourself".

How to ask a question in a way that gives us the best result?

Many people don't only have a problem asking questions, but once they exceed that threshold, they have a problem with asking a direct question. "Direct" in the meaning of: making a request to the person that has the authority to make a decision. It has nothing to do with an open or closed question so don't get confused.

I have some good news for the people fearing to address a person in a direct way: the best question in networking is an "indirect" one!

Let's take a look where this "best question" comes from.

Step 1: from a "direct" to an "indirect" question

For example, instead of asking: "Will you hire me as a marketing assistant?" you can ask: "Do you know anyone that is looking for a new marketing assistant?"

If this person is looking for a new marketing assistant, he will tell you. If not, you have **triggered his mind into thinking of other people who might be able to help you**.

Another benefit of this question is that you give the other person the possibility to say "no" to your request (hiring you) without jeopardizing the relationship between the two of you. You give him the opportunity to help you in another way: introducing you to someone else or giving you other tips to reach your goal.

Step 2: from an "indirect" question to the best question in networking

The previous "indirect" question is already a huge step in the right direction. But the "best question" would be: "Who do you think I should contact when looking for a new job as marketing assistant?"

This way you don't only ask an indirect question, but you also have the possibility to **receive a whole list of good contacts that may refer you to people from their network**. You also broaden your possibilities. Maybe your contact doesn't know any marketing directors, but one of his best friends could be the editor of a marketing magazine.

In other words, the best and safest question to ask your network is:

> **"Who do you think I should contact with respect to ..."**
> **+ your specific question**

You would be surprised of the results of this approach. Do me and especially yourself a favor and try it!

To encourage you to really do this, I want to share this story with you:

In July 2005 I had lunch with change management consultant Han Juch of AlterMate. He told me that my advice about approaching people had worked. In the past he had difficulties to get appointments with potential customers. But now he had contacted some companies to ask them if they knew someone who would benefit from his specific experience in setting up and maintaining "the second organization," a specific concept of him about change management. The companies he contacted "lowered their guard" and were willing to listen to his story and to help him look for customers. After his meetings, two of the three companies he visited were interested themselves in his concept and his experiences at other companies. And they wanted to introduce him to people from their network as well!

> **Networking success tip:** if you want to move ahead in your professional and personal life *and* give your network the opportunity to assist you, it is important to ask regularly and in a respectful way!

LinkedIn provides many tools to ask questions like the "Answers" and "Discussions" functionality. Also the "Status Update" feature can be used for this. How to use these tools will be described in a later chapter.

Thank

Most of us do thank people when we received something or when someone delivered a solution to a problem. But do we always thank people if we did NOT get something? Do you always thank someone when she took the time to look for a solution, but didn't find one? Or when she just took the time to listen to you?

Maybe you also recognize the following story. One of the things I still have difficulties with myself is remembering to thank people who introduced or referred me a long time ago. Let me explain this a little more. In January 2005 I got the name of a contact person at company X from a networking contact. They were interested in training their people in networking. Time went by and there were a few contacts, but still no course. Until December. Then I got the phone call where my contact asked me to do a networking training course for his company.

I'm a bit ashamed to admit that I forgot to thank the initiator of this contact. But it's so important to do this, even when months go by and lots of other projects and events intervene. Just by doing this small effort, you strengthen the relationship and keep your contact involved in your successes. This way he is encouraged to help you even more. To avoid this in the future we now keep track of all the introductions we received. When a project finally starts the referrers receive a small gift to show our gratitude.

In a next chapter you will read how to use LinkedIn to thank people.

Fundamental Principle 3: The Real Power of the Network is in the Second Degree

When people think about networking and how it can help them they think: I have to have the right people in my network. Your own network is called your first degree network (on LinkedIn you also see the number 1 next to the name of a person to whom you are connected yourself).

Thinking that the power of the network is in the first degree is one of the largest barriers for people to really achieve their goals.

The real power of the network is not in who you know, but in who they know. The real power of the network is in the second degree. There are many more opportunities there.

Of course you need the first degree to reach the second degree, so the first degree is still very important.

Understanding that the real power of networking is in the second degree also helps to deal with your network and the people you meet in a different way. You don't have to do business with them. You don't have to "sell" yourself to them.

If you understand that the power of the network is in the second degree you can have other kinds of conversations. You can take the time to get to know each other a little bit better and see how you can help each other towards each other's network.

How many people do you meet that you think: "No matter how nice this person is, I will never do business with him or her because we are in totally different industries, geographic areas or functions. Let's end this conversation as fast as I can so I can start talking to someone who is really interesting to me."

But you never know who they know. If you make time to have a longer conversation, ask them what or who they are looking for and share what your goals are, you might be very surprised.

Also by getting the "direct or hard selling" part out of the way (and this doesn't only apply to sales people but also to people looking for a new job or a new employee) with the person you are talking to, networking becomes more relaxed and more fun.

One of the biggest advantages of LinkedIn is that it helps to leverage this power of the second degree. What makes LinkedIn the fantastic tool it is, is that it shows you the network of your network. LinkedIn shows the second and third degree contacts together with ALL the connections you have with them

Understanding this concept and being able to apply it, will be the single most important success factor for you on LinkedIn. To help you really grasp this concept we will do a small exercise in the chapter "Experience the Power of LinkedIn"

Fundamental Principle 4: Quality and Diversity are both Important

There are always many discussions about what is most important in networking: quality or quantity. In "Let's Connect!" I wrote about this discussion. Since it is pretty fundamental I repeat it here and then discuss the strength of weak links.

Actually the discussion is about a "wrong" topic. It is not quantity that is important, but diversity. The consequence, however, is that the more diverse your network is, the more people will be in it.

Let's look at both quality and diversity a little bit closer.

The Importance of Quality

Let me start by asking you a question: what is quality? How do you define it?

Many people perceive people with a high position in a large and well-known company as "high quality". Let's call such a person Ms. Big Shot. And they do everything they can to come into contact with her when they see her at an event. But when they get a few minutes of this person's attention they don't know what to say and focus on exchanging business cards. Afterwards they send emails and start calling Ms. Big Shot, only to be blocked by her secretary. And then they are disappointed in Ms. Big Shot, the event where they attended and in networking in general.

Do you recognize this situation? From your own experience or from someone you know? Then it might be a good idea to look differently at "quality".

For me "quality" can only be measured when compared to your goals. A person is of "high quality" if she (or her network) can help you to reach your goals better and faster. Ms. Big Shot could be high quality, but she is also very busy. So it might be a good idea to look for other people of equal quality that are easier to approach and who have more time for you.

So quality is definitely important in networking. But so is diversity. Why?

The Importance of Diversity

There are 4 major reasons why diversity is important.

Your goals change over time

As your goals change over time, the "quality" of people changes too. Somebody who was of "low quality" a year ago could be number one today. Also the opposite is true. So this is another reason why everybody is important.

For example: a former product manager of a large telecom company told me that he was never interested in meeting accountants and lawyers at events of the Chamber of Commerce. Moreover, he ran away from them. But at the moment he started his own company, he regretted the fact that he didn't have any connections in those two fields.

More opportunities

A more diverse and larger network gives you more opportunities to find the "high quality" people. But again, this means that you have to know your goals. I'm not a promoter of collecting as many contacts as you possibly can. At events and on the Internet you will see many people expanding their (virtual) address books. For some of them it's kind of a sport. To be able to brag: "look at how many people I know." But when one of these contacts wants to deepen the relationship, they don't answer emails or phone calls. Don't get me wrong. There is nothing wrong with huge address books. As long as you are available to your network. On the other hand if you're just collecting people like collecting stamps, it might be good to tell them that. This way there are no wrong expectations. Wrong expectations can harm your reputation. And that's the last thing you want in networking.

Having more opportunities also means that you have to rely less on luck or coincidence for things to happen in your life. Lots of contacts combined with knowing your goals will have you experience more synchronicity in your life too!

Value for your network

Somebody might be of "low quality" for you, but of "high quality" for someone from your network. A good networking action is connecting people. By connecting them, you strengthen your relationship with both of them. This creates goodwill. They will both be more motivated to help you to find the "high quality" people you are looking for.

In fact, connecting people is one of the best networking actions you can do. It is free, doesn't cost much time and you help two people at the same time. You will be remembered as a great help and as a consequence the chances increase that they will remember you when there is an opportunity in your field of expertise or when you reach out for help.

Diversity creates a larger safety net when circumstances change

We all have the tendency to stick around people who have the same interests, the same background, the same education and other similar things. Wayne Baker calls this the "similarity principle." In his book "Networking Smart" you find many examples of this principle. Sometimes this tendency to stick around with the same people is good, sometimes it is a disadvantage. For example, when you are looking for a new job, it is better to have a large and diversified network. This is what is called "the strength of weak links". Your small core group will limit you to the same sources of information or job opportunities.

Find your Balance between Quality and Diversity

You now know that diversity and quality are both important.

So what should you do next? It's a cliché, but my advice is:

Find your own balance between quality and diversity.

Remember that a person that is not "interesting" for you today might become very helpful towards your next goal. And besides, you never know who this person knows or how he could help somebody from your network.

For example: when I was gathering input for this book many people I won't ever sell to or buy from helped me to post a request for input on LinkedIn Groups. In that way they helped me to get input from people I wouldn't have been able to reach myself.

In a later chapter we will see how both strong and weak ties on LinkedIn can help us effectively reach our goals and reach them faster as well.

Fundamental Principle 5: Your "Know, Like and Trust" Factor

Networking and referral expert Bob Burg is famous for his quote (from the excellent book "Endless Referrals"): **"All things being equal, people do business with, and refer business to people they know, like and trust."**

So in order to build relationships it is important to raise your Know factor, your Like factor and your Trust factor with the people from your network.

What does this mean in practice?

- **Know factor**: what do people know about you? What is your background? What are your interests on a professional and personal level? Which organizations do you belong to? To raise your Know factor it is important to fill in your Profile on LinkedIn as much as you can. Tips on how to do this will be given in a next chapter.

- **Like factor**: people like other people who are helpful, kind and not pushy. Applying the networking attitude, thinking about what you can share with other people and answering questions in Discussions and Answers already helps a lot to raise your Like factor. More tips about how to do this on LinkedIn follow in a next chapter.

- **Trust factor**: there are two kinds of trust:

  o **Trust that you are an expert**. This part of the trust factor can be raised when answering questions in Answers and Discussions in your field of expertise. By giving good and solid answers you will be perceived as the expert. Also by having recommendations from other people describing your *professional expertise* your Trust factor will increase.

  o **Trust that you will behave in a decent way** when you get an introduction or referral. This is a consequence of your behavior described in the Like factor. Having recommendations from other people describing your *attitude* when working with them will also raise this part of the Trust factor.

LinkedIn helps to raise your Know, Like and Trust factor in many ways. As Stephen M.R. Covey wrote in his book, "The Speed of Trust": trust can also be transferred from one person to another. Therefore, it is good to ask for introductions and to pass on messages when you trust people; this is one of the best and easiest networking actions to take. It also works the other way around: trust (and your reputation) can be damaged very quickly. So don't only be a good advocate, but also a good filter!

The Challenge

By now you understand that starting from goals makes it lots easier to start (online) networking and to tap into the power of your network to get results. You also learned about the 5 fundamental principles behind networking.

The challenge now is to combine both. If you only focus on your goals and don't use the 5 fundamental principles it will be much harder to get results. You also will get many negative reactions if you only use your network, but don't reciprocate.

The consequence is that it will require some effort from you to help people and to make time to connect your contacts to each other. This might appear to some as time consuming. But if you start expanding your network with your goals in mind and use LinkedIn as a tool in the way it is described in this book, this strategy will get you results so much faster that you save much more time than you have to put into it.

Conclusion of this chapter

(Online) networking is the most powerful and free resource everybody has. To really get results, starting from a goal is key. Understanding and applying the fundamental principles of networking will make you succeed in both networking online, on the phone and in all your face-to-face contacts. As a reminder, these are the 5 fundamental principles:

1. Networking attitude: sharing information in a reactive and proactive way without expecting anything in return immediately.

2. The Golden Triangle of Networking: Give (or Share), Ask and Thank.

3. The Real Power of the Network is in the Second Degree.

4. Quality and Diversity are both important.

5. Your Know, Like and Trust Factor will be taken into account when dealing with people. Make sure all three factors are high.

In the next chapters you will learn how to build a successful online networking strategy on LinkedIn on these 5 fundamental principles.

LinkedIn: What Is It and How Could I Benefit from It?

Since you bought this book chances are that you already have a Profile on LinkedIn and had at least some first experiences with this online business networking platform. Or you might be using LinkedIn on a regular basis and want to get more out of it.

For either type it is good to take a moment and look at what LinkedIn is and what it is not, what the single most important benefit of LinkedIn is and how it can improve your (business) life as well.

What is LinkedIn?

At the moment of writing (December 2008) LinkedIn is the largest online **business** network website worldwide with more than 32 million users and growing fast (the last year LinkedIn grew from 19 million users to 32 million, depending on when you read this book this might already have doubled or tripled again). There are people from all industries and a large variation of job titles and it is used by high level profiles (for example, executives of all Fortune 500 companies are members). The average age is 41, which makes it already from a demographic point of view different from Facebook, which is internationally the most used social networking website with more than 150 million users and an average age of 20 (in the USA MySpace is still the largest platform). LinkedIn is a platform to give you visibility, connect with others, help others and be helped by them.

Although some people think it is a sales tool, for me LinkedIn is a networking platform: it is a platform to start and maintain relationships. The consequence of building relationships might be a sale, but also a new job, finding a new employee, supplier, partner or expertise.

Some people don't agree with me (and I'm fine with that ☺). They have a sales or recruiting goal and they just use LinkedIn and other networking websites for that. And they have results. But not as much as they might have. By shortcutting fundamental principles 1, 2 and 5 (networking attitude, Golden Triangle of Networking and the know, like and trust factor) they lose many opportunities. They spend lots of time without getting the results they might have.

LinkedIn (and other tools) is also not more and certainly not less than that: a powerful tool to start and build relationships. A tool is something you use to support you, not a goal. When you see the amount of connections that some people have, you might have a different idea about that, but for me LinkedIn is only a tool, but a very powerful one.

It is also one of the many tools we have nowadays at our disposal in the whole Social Media spectrum. Other members of this "family" are blogs, wikis (Wikipedia), microblogging (Twitter), Photosharing (Flickr), Videosharing (Youtube) and social bookmarking (Delicious). What is interesting to see is that they all grow towards each other as well. LinkedIn started this integration in November 2008 when they launched Applications which allows, for example, to show your blog posts or slideshows in your Profile.

Erwin Van Lun, futurist and trend analyst, goes even a step further when describing LinkedIn:

"LinkedIn is an essential part of the new economy. LinkedIn is not just a handy website or a tool to leverage your business, communicate with other people or find contacts. No, LinkedIn shows the foundation of an open, networked system that arises when we have cleaned up the capitalistic, closed system. In such a world new companies help people as a virtual coach in several domains. LinkedIn specializes in the "work" domain.

This evolution in the new economy started with contacts, jobs and events. Then education, job orientation or mediation. When you project this to LinkedIn, you notice LinkedIn has just started. LinkedIn will evolve to a reliable companion in the whole work niche. Worldwide. LinkedIn is just at the beginning."

Just like Erwin I'm very curious how LinkedIn is going to develop and how it can help us in our (business) lives even more than it does now. Watch Erwin's blog for his view on LinkedIn and other trends: www.erwinvanlun.com

The single most important benefit of LinkedIn

For me the most powerful concept behind LinkedIn is that it **finds the right people AND the connections you have with them**. It makes the networks of the people we know visible. LinkedIn shows us our second and third degree networks and the paths towards them. This has tremendous value.

Why? Many people already have difficulty keeping track of their own (first degree) network. It is impossible to know who our network knows. LinkedIn makes this visible. This is extremely powerful especially if you start with the end or goal in mind. Many people make the "mistake" to only look in their own network when they are looking for someone to help them. In this way they are limiting themselves tremendously.

What if we start with defining the best person, find them and then find out via whom we can get introduced to them?

For example let's suppose you are looking for a job at Coca Cola in your country (or you want to do business with them as a supplier or partner).

What most people then do is think of who they might know at Coca Cola. Then they can't think of anyone and give up. Or they call the front desk, ask for the HR Manager and are stalled by the receptionist. Or the HR Manager says she is going to call back, but never does. Frustration!

Let's now start with the goal in mind. You define the HR Manager as the person who can help you best reaching your goal (a job, a contract or expertise). Then you use LinkedIn and do a search with "HR Manager, Coca Cola, and your country". The result is that you don't only find the exact name of the person, but also the connections you share with this person.

When you then look at the mutual connections you have, you might discover that this person is connected with your neighbor. You didn't know this because Coca Cola never has come up in your conversations. He has never mentioned anything about it and you never told him that you were interested in working for or with Coca Cola. After discovering the connection on LinkedIn and talking to your neighbor about it, you find out that he has worked together with the HR Manager in the past. When he hears about your goal he agrees on writing an email to introduce you to the HR Manager. Five days later you are invited to have a talk with the HR Manager and land the job or contract.

Without LinkedIn you might never have known that they knew each other!

Of course not everybody is on LinkedIn yet, so you won't find every person or function you are looking for. However. LinkedIn is a website focused on business networking. What this means in practice is that we are able to find many people and access to most organizations. What we see in practice is that the majority of organizations are represented on LinkedIn (as already mentioned in the USA, all of the Fortune 500 companies have an executive level presence). Maybe you don't find the Marketing Manager of a company, but you might find the IT Manager. The Marketing Manager is only one step away from him. OK, it is some extra effort, but still lots easier than before LinkedIn existed.

An extra advantage of being connected with people on LinkedIn that many users have reported is that you always have their most up-to-date email address.

How could LinkedIn benefit you?

As already mentioned LinkedIn is a tool that supports the networking process. So it supports all the benefits we already mentioned in the previous chapter.

To make it more clear how it can benefit you in your specific role, let's start with summing up the benefits per "task". This will make it more clear to you how you, in your situation, can benefit from it.

In the next chapter you will be presented with a basic strategy that applies to everybody. In a later chapter you will get an advanced strategy geared towards each task separately.

Benefit / Task	Find New Customers	Find a Job or Internship	Find Suppliers or Partners	Find Employees	How does LinkedIn help with this?
Identifying the right people					Find their profile via search or browse.
Discovering information about ...					Reading their Profile before a meeting.
Maintaining relationship with ...	Prospects and customers	Recruiters or HR responsibles	Suppliers or Partners	Candidates	Personal messages, sharing ideas in Discussions and answering questions in Answers.
Getting recommendations which are visible to everybody, but especially to ...					Recommendations.
Receiving introductions or referrals to ...	Prospects and other departments at current customer	Recruiters or HR responsibles	Suppliers or Partners	Candidates	Via the introductions tool or outside LinkedIn (Email).

Benefit / Task	Find New Customers	Find a Job or Internship	Find Suppliers or Partners	Find Employees	How does LinkedIn help with this?
Discovering the relationships between …	Customers, prospects and other contacts.	Recruiters, HR responsibles and other contacts.	Suppliers or Partners and other contacts.	Candidates and other contacts.	Via the connections in their Profile.
	Your colleagues from the same and other departments and prospects*.	Your fellow students or job seekers and potential employers.	Your colleagues from the same and other departments and potential suppliers and partners.	Your colleagues from the same and other departments and potential employees.	
Visibility, Personal Branding and Online Reputation of …	You as a sales (wo)man and your company.	You	You and your company	You as a recruiter and your company	Your Profile not only on LinkedIn, but also in the Search Engines like Google, contributions in Answers and in Discussions.
Word of mouth publicity	People writing about you so your prospects might hear about you.	People writing about you so your new employer might hear about you.	People writing about you so potential suppliers or partners might hear about you.	People writing about you so your candidates might hear about you.	Receiving recommendations and people telling about you in Discussions, mention you as the expert in Answers or talking about you outside of LinkedIn.

*: This might avoid painful situations when sales people from the same company call the same prospect or customer without knowing that their colleagues from the same or a different department are already in touch with them.

Benefit / Task	Find New Customers	Find a Job or Internship	Find Suppliers or Partners	Find Employees	How does LinkedIn help with this?
Getting notifications when someone changes jobs, this is a trigger to contact them to see if ...	You can be a supplier to the new organization and to get introduced to the one who will replace them at your current customer.	Their new job is recruiter or HR responsible or if (s)he is going to work for the organization you want to work for.	They can become a supplier or partner.	Someone suddenly qualifies for a job opening.	Via Network Updates.
Picking up trends in the marketplace via Discussions in Groups of ...	Customers and prospects.	Sector where you want to work in.	Suppliers or Partners	Candidates.	Discussions.
	Other sales people.		Your peers.	Other recruiters.	
Make yourself be perceived as an expert			You		Contributions in Discussions and Answers (can lead to Expert points).
Finding the Groups and organizations to be member of, both online and offline which are right for ...			You		Via Group Search and via the Profiles of people from your network.

Extra benefits:

- **For sales**: Getting notifications via Network Updates when your customers link with sales reps from a company that offers the same products or services than yours. This might be a trigger to contact your customers again.

- **For job seekers**: LinkedIn offers extra tools to help you. For example, you can react very easily to job postings and use an extra job tool in your browser when surfing any website.

- **For recruiters**: LinkedIn offers extra tools to help you. For example to post a job on LinkedIn and to do a reference search.

Get your project or job more effectively and efficiently done

If the above topics don't apply to you, you have probably an "internal function". Or you may "wear several hats" and have an external and internal role at the same time.

Although many people who only have an internal function don't think networking in general and LinkedIn specifically is useful to them, LinkedIn can also bring many benefits to them. The most important one is that although many larger organizations have their own telephone and email directories, the information is very basic and limited to practical details. When people fill in their Profile on LinkedIn their colleagues might not only discover more about them, which allows better forming of teams, but also who is in their network.

As far as I know, there is no organization in the world which has that knowledge in an internal system. It is also very hard to do because they would have to ask every employee to list their connections and also update them when something changes. Since most people don't have enough time to do their normal work, this is the first thing they will stop doing. The basic principle behind LinkedIn and any other social or business network is that everybody updates their own profile. You can never make this work in an internal system.

A last remark is that people who get things done, get more visibility, get promoted faster and will be the last ones to get fired. Getting things done also means that the job needs to be done, not that you have to do everything yourself. Finding the right people is crucial in this new economy of specialists.

So if you have an "internal function", LinkedIn can bring these benefits to you:

1. Getting answers to your questions (via Answers or Discussions)

2. Receiving introductions or referrals to colleagues. This is especially helpful when you are forming a team as a project leader or want to be part of a team in a large organization (via the introductions tool or outside LinkedIn via email or telephone)

3. Identifying the experts inside your company (finding their Profile via a search or via the Expert rating)

4. Visibility for your own strengths and expertise + Personal Branding or Online Reputation (your Profile, contributions in Answers and in Discussions)

5. Identifying the right colleagues in your own department, in other departments or in another state or country (finding their Profile)

6. Discovering the relationships between your colleagues from the same and other departments (see the connections in their Profiles)

7. Discovering information about colleagues which makes the conversations online and offline easier (reading their Profile)

8. Maintaining relationship with colleagues, especially when they are in offices in a different location (Personal contacts, Discussions in Groups and answering questions in Answers)

9. Make yourself be perceived as an expert (contributions in Answers and in Discussions and Expert points)

10. Word of mouth publicity (receiving Recommendations and people telling about you in Discussions, mention you as the expert in Answers or talking about you outside of LinkedIn)

11. Getting Recommendations (Recommendations written by other people which can't be modified by you on LinkedIn which makes them stronger)

12. Finding the right groups and organizations to be member of, both online and offline. For example, alumni groups, women's groups or colleagues with the same function (via the Profiles of people from your network)

13. Picking up trends in the marketplace (Discussions in the Groups of your peers)

14. Getting notifications when someone changes jobs, this is a trigger to contact them to see if they can be on your next team or you on theirs and to get introduced to the one who will replace them (via Network Updates)

Increase the amount of members of your (professional) organization

Many (professional) organizations have a hard time to keep their organization interesting enough for their members and are also continuously looking to attract new members.

Starting your own LinkedIn Group can both add to the value of the membership and attract more members in many ways:

1. An online presence next to events will help members to keep in touch between meetings.

2. Members who can't attend many meetings will still be able to contact each other.

3. The LinkedIn Group is an extra platform to help each other and to discuss trends.

4. Some potential members might have never heard of your organization. They can get in touch with you and become a member of your organization after finding the LinkedIn Group.

5. It is a good and free alternative to a forum on your own website. Many organizations have a hard time building a successful community because they don't have a critical mass of people who participate in discussions. As a result, people won't visit the forum anymore, the negative spiral continues and they also hardly ever visit the website anymore. Since people use LinkedIn to connect with other people and to build their network with other people than the members of your organization, they will keep using LinkedIn and once in a while visit the LinkedIn Group of your organization.

6. Free membership of the LinkedIn Group might generate interest in a (paid) membership for events.

Conclusion of this chapter

LinkedIn is a business network that has exponentially grown over the past few years. The single most important reason why to use LinkedIn is that it helps you not only find the people who can help you reach your goals, but also the mutual contacts who can introduce you to them.

LinkedIn offers many benefits for every profile: finding new customers, a new job, new employees, suppliers, partners, expertise internal or external to your company and other information to get your job done faster.

Among many other things LinkedIn helps with discovering relationships between people, getting access, introductions and referrals to the people you are looking for, getting answers to your questions, raising your visibility, finding the right groups to be a member of both on LinkedIn and in real life, getting notifications when someone changes jobs, discussing issues and picking up trends in the market place.

Also for people who run professional organizations or associations LinkedIn helps to stimulate the interaction between members and attract more members.

So now you know what LinkedIn can do for you, let's look at the features LinkedIn has.

LinkedIn: Functionality

Now that we know what the fundamental principles of networking are, what LinkedIn is and how it can benefit you, let's look at the main functionality as our last building block before we start with building an effective LinkedIn strategy. We will look at the 7 major parts of LinkedIn on the left hand side and the 4 major parts at the top and explain briefly what they do.

If you have already been using LinkedIn for a while, you might be tempted to skip this chapter. However, I would suggest not to do that. In this chapter I will also share some interesting details, which can help you to use LinkedIn even better or more efficiently.

This is the most "dangerous" chapter of the book since the functionality and look of LinkedIn might have changed between the moment I have written this chapter and the moment you read it.

In the next chapter we will then start with our online strategy. That is also where we go into the details of the LinkedIn functionality.

Now is a good time to log in to LinkedIn and experience yourself what I'm writing about.

One remark: in LinkedIn terms your network consists of your first three degrees. People who are further away from you are considered "out of your network".

The Left Hand Menu

Home

Your Home Page is the page you see when you log in on LinkedIn. It is a portal page with messages and updates from people from your network.

Most of the time people don't really look at this page because they are triggered via email when someone contacts them, but it might be interesting to look a little bit more in detail to this page.

On the main page there are two columns. Let's start with the one on the left:

- **Inbox:** the last 5 messages, which you haven't responded on.

- **Network Updates**: Connection Updates, Status Updates, Group Updates, Questions & Answers and Profile Updates. These are all updates about one person from your network. It can be interesting to look at this to have a reason to get back in touch with someone, or that you know that your contact person at a certain company leaves so you have to take immediate action to get in touch with the person who replaces him.

- **Other Group Updates**: when something changes in a Group you belong to (new members, new discussion,...)

- **Just Joined LinkedIn**: colleagues and classmates, which are related to your Profile. Easy to find classmates and colleagues without having to search for them every day yourself. It is good to get back in touch with them because they have already had an experience with you and will be more inclined to give you a recommendation. To strengthen your relationship with them you might share some tips from this book to give them a jump-start. Since they are new to LinkedIn they might have many questions about how to use it. By helping them out yourself or pointing them to this book or the blog you can start by sharing something without expecting anything in return.

The column on the right hand side contains:

- **People you may know**: LinkedIn suggests some people you may know. How does LinkedIn calculate this? From the FAQ pages of LinkedIn: *"The feature works by looking for common attributes between individuals (e.g. same company, industry or school) and makes a prediction on likelihood that you might know that person. Note these are only suggestions."*

- An advertisement. Unfortunately you can't get rid of it ☺

- **Who's viewed my Profile**: some statistics about people who have visited your Profile. Sometimes you will see who it was, sometimes only a description. Where does the difference come from? It depends what that person has filled in himself in his "Account & Settings" under "Privacy Settings" and then "Profile Views". Standard of this is: "Only show my anonymous Profile characteristics, such as industry and title". Since only a few people change their settings, this is what you will see most of the time when people have looked at your Profile. In other words, you will only rarely see the actual name.

- **Events**: a box with a search and browse function to find events, which might be interesting for you. When you click on the "Browse Events for you" link you go the Events page. On that page you can not only find events you might be interested in, but also add your own event. I assume LinkedIn will do more with this Event functionality in the future.

- **Other applications like Answers, Jobs, People and Applications**: these are small applications that you can customize to your own needs. You can delete the ones you don't want. You can also add some extra applications. For example, I have three Answers applications on my Home Page. One about the topic "Using LinkedIn", one about "Professional Networking" and one about "Professional Development". These are areas where my expertise can help other people and where I would like to increase my visibility. By adding these applications I'm alerted when a question is posted. I might have missed it otherwise.

As you can see there is some interesting information on the Home Page, so spend a little more time looking at it the next time you log on!

Groups

A rather new part of LinkedIn is dedicated to Groups. Actually, Groups were already there for a while, but LinkedIn is adding more and more functionality to this part of the website. I'm very happy that they are doing this because it makes the website even more valuable.

Under "Groups" there are three main options:

- My Groups: overview of the Groups you are member of
- Groups Directory (with search and browse functionality)
- Create a Group: when you want to start your own Group.

In each Group these options are available (some can be turned off by the Group Manager):

- Overview: portal page of the Group with a summary of all the other items
- Discussions: questions and answers from Group members
- News: links (to articles) posted inside this Group
- Updates: messages
- Members: overview of the members of this Group
- Settings:
  - Visibility settings: display logo of Group on your Profile or not
  - Contact settings: receive digest email from the Group or not (+ frequency), allow members of the Group to contact you through LinkedIn or not

- Group Profile: description of the Group
- Manage: only visible for Group Managers

Your Profile

Networking on LinkedIn starts with making your own Profile. This is your representation on LinkedIn. It will help you to create visibility and to be found by other people. So it is important to give enough attention when creating it.

Does it have to be right, perfect and 100% complete at once? No, you can start with a simple Profile and then add more details to it later. People's lives are not static; they are dynamic, so keep updating your Profile every time something noteworthy happens.

LinkedIn provides you with two Profiles:

- **Your Profile on LinkedIn**, which can only be viewed by other members of LinkedIn who are within three degrees from you and to people with premium accounts.

- **Your Public Profile** which can be seen by everyone and which can also be found via search engines like Google, Yahoo and MSN Live Search. You control which parts of your Profile are included in the Public Profile.

LinkedIn has a built-in functionality to show how "complete" your Profile is. And also how much percentage each part of information contributes to reach 100%.

Under Profile you also find the tools to accept recommendations from others, decide whether or not to show them, to give recommendations to others and to ask for recommendations.

In the next chapter we will cover more in depth the different aspects of the Profile together with some do's and don'ts.

Contacts

A network is only a network when there are connections with other people.

Under "Contacts" you can look at your current connections. From this page you can also import and add connections and remove connections.

Note: you can filter your connections in three ways: people with new connections, by location and by industry.

You can also look at the Network Statistics from this page: you can see how many people are in your first, second and third degree network and in the whole network. Other information you can find on this page is regional access (what are the top 5 areas your connections are from) and industry access (what are the top 5 industries your connections are from).

Inbox

Under "Inbox" you will retrieve all of your messages that you have received and sent. These received and sent messages can be found in two ways:

- All together when clicking on "Inbox". You will then see a header "Action Items". Here you will find all the invitations and other messages you have received for which you haven't taken action (which means in practice: accepted/declined, replied or archived). After taking any action LinkedIn automatically transfers it to the specific category it belongs to.

- Under different categories: messages, InMails, introductions, Invitations, Profiles, Q&A, Jobs, Recommendations and Groups. A special category is Network Updates.

Although you can send messages from the Inbox our experience is that not many people take actions via the Inbox unless they want to ask some people from their first degree network a question. They take actions from within Groups, when they are on someone's Profile or when responding to questions in Answers or Discussions. But it's good to know there is a place where you can find everything back.

Applications

At the time of writing this is a brand new section on LinkedIn. In this section you can integrate one or more applications like a blog or a slideshow with your LinkedIn Profile. A very interesting feature.

These are the applications that were available when LinkedIn started offering applications (the explanation of each application comes from the LinkedIn website, I added the categories):

Reading lists

- **Reading List by Amazon:** Extend your professional Profile by sharing the books you're reading with other LinkedIn members. Find out what you should be reading by following updates from your connections, people in your field, or other LinkedIn members of professional interest to you.

Blogs

- **WordPress:** Connect your virtual lives with the WordPress LinkedIn Application. With the WordPress App, you can sync your WordPress blog posts with your LinkedIn Profile, keeping everyone you know in the know.

- **Blog Link**: With Blog Link, you can get the most of your LinkedIn relationships by connecting your blog to your LinkedIn Profile. Blog Link helps you, and your professional network, stay connected.

Polls

- **LinkedIn Polls**: The Polls application is a market research tool that allows you to collect actionable data from your connections and the professional audience on LinkedIn.

Presentations and files

- **SlideShare presentations**: SlideShare is the best way to share presentations on LinkedIn! You can upload and display your own presentations, check out presentations from your colleagues, and find experts within your network.

- **Google Presentation**: Present yourself and your work. Upload a .PPT or use Google's online application to embed a presentation on your Profile.

Online collaboration

- **Box.net files**: Add the Box.net Files application to manage all your important files online. Box.net lets you share content on your Profile, and collaborate with friends and colleagues.

- **Huddle Workspaces**: Huddle gives you private, secure online workspaces packed with simple yet powerful project, collaboration and sharing tools for working with your connections.

Market watch

- **Company Buzz**: Ever wonder what people are saying about your company? Company Buzz shows you the Twitter activity associated with your company. View tweets (the messages sent via Twitter), trends and top key words. Customize your topics and share with your co-workers.

Travel / location sharing

- **My Travel**: See where your LinkedIn network is traveling and when you will be in the same city as your colleagues. Share your upcoming trips, current location, and travel stats with your network.

As you can see there are already a lot of applications and I expect more to come. The integration seems to work pretty good (but I haven't tested all applications). For my blog it only took me 20 seconds to get it integrated with my LinkedIn Profile (by the way I'm using WordPress as blog tool).

Why are these applications interesting? Because they can help you raise your visibility and help other people. Remember the networking attitude and the first angle of the Golden Triangle of networking from the first chapter. These applications allow you to easily share your expertise with your network.

Add Connections

The last function on the left hand side is the green button "Add Connections".

When you click at this button, you will see that there are several ways to add connections to your network from within LinkedIn:

- **Invite contacts**: you can invite 6 contacts by typing in their first name, last name and email address. Underneath the box you will see "Edit/Preview Invitation Text". **Always make sure to click on it and replace the standard invitation text with a personal one!**

- **Import contacts**: you can also import contacts from Outlook or Webmail applications like Gmail, Hotmail, Yahoo and AOL. Good to know is that the contacts you have imported will appear under "Contacts/Imported Contacts". No one else but you can see this. You still have to send them an invitation to connect from within "Imported Contacts". A small note: when upgrading to Windows Vista this function didn't work anymore on my computer. Luckily the LinkedIn help pages came to my rescue. This is what you need to do when you get a processing error when you use Vista and Internet Explorer 7 (from the LinkedIn Help pages):

    Security settings on Internet Explorer 7 running on Windows Vista may cause you to receive the following error: 'There was an error processing your request'. To upload your contacts you will need to modify your Security settings.

- *Open Internet Explorer 7.*

- *Go to 'Tools' and choose 'Internet Options'.*

- *Select the 'Security' tab.*

- *Select the 'Internet' zone.*

- *Disable/uncheck the checkbox called 'Enable Protected Mode'.*

- *Click 'Apply', then 'OK' until you exit this dialog.*

- *Restart IE 7 - The status bar at the bottom should now state 'Internet | Protected Mode: Off'.*

- *Retry uploading your contacts to LinkedIn.*

- **Colleagues**: you can find current and past colleagues. LinkedIn uses the information about the companies you have worked for in your Profile and matches that with the information about the companies other LinkedIn members have worked for.

- **Classmates**: you can find current and past classmates. LinkedIn uses the information about the schools in your Profile and matches that with the information about the schools other LinkedIn members have listed. You even get more options: find people back who have studied during the same years as you or have graduated in the same year.

You can also invite contacts directly from Outlook. We will discuss that option in the chapter about the extra tools.

Menu at the top

People

Under "People" you will find the option, which is used the most on LinkedIn: the search option. The most used search is the simple search on every keyword from a Profile, which you see at the top on the right hand side of almost every page on LinkedIn.

Next to this search you will find two other searches when you click on "People":

- Advanced People Search: you can use several parameters in your search
- Reference Search: allows you to retrieve people who worked for a specific company during a specific time period. This allows finding,

for example, colleagues of someone you want to hire. To be able to look at the details of this function, you have to upgrade your free account.

Jobs

Since this is very specific for people looking for a job or recruiters who want to fill a position, this functionality is discussed more in detail in the Advanced Strategies chapter for those profiles.

Answers

Under "Answers" there are 5 categories:

1. Answers Home: portal page of the Answers section

2. Advanced Answers Search: find questions or answers using keywords and categories. You can search on open and closed questions. This is a good place to start to look before asking a new question.

3. My Q&A: overview of public and private questions you have asked and answered.

4. Ask a question: when you ask a question, give enough details. Use the title, details and categorize options and specify whether your question is linked to a specific geographic region or not.

5. Answer Questions: you can browse through open questions, closed questions and experts or browse via categories.

Companies

Under "Companies" there are two options: Companies and Service Providers.

Let's look at Companies first:

*   To find a company, you can search or browse on industry, search on name and you also get an overview of companies in your first degree network.

*   If you are looking for a larger company you can find some interesting information and statistics:

- Who from your first and second degree works for that company: interesting starting point if you want to do business with this company.

- **New Hires**: if you see which kind of profiles they are hiring and at which rate you might see some business opportunities.

- **Recent Promotions and Changes**: if you see that your key contact has changed position you can take immediate action to be introduced to the person who replaces him. Or if you weren't able to get in touch with the old sales manager, you might have a chance with the new one.

- **Popular Profiles**: it might be interesting to see who they are and which role they play officially and off the record for their company.

- **Related Companies**

  - **Divisions**: if the current company is already a customer, their divisions might be additional customers. It always surprises me how many times the wheel is reinvented, and how poor communication about suppliers is between departments and divisions. The bigger the organization, the more true this is. So use LinkedIn to find the people in these other divisions and then ask for an introduction or referral. If you are looking for a job at the mother company, it might also be interesting to find out whether the divisions are looking for someone or whether someone from a division might introduce you to someone from the mother company.

  - **Career Path for employees of this company** (before and after): see remark for divisions.

  - **Employees of this company are most connected to**: see remark for divisions.

- **Key Statistics**: number of people working for this company, common job titles, top schools, median age, percentage male/female

Under "Service Providers" there are three options:

- **Services Home**:

  - Who gets into this directory? Everybody who has received at least one recommendation.

o   You can see who is recommended by you, by your first degree network, by your second degree network and by the whole LinkedIn Network. You can also browse through categories.

o   This is a good place to start if you are looking for a supplier or partner. Most people, however, use the search function.

- **Make a recommendation**: recommend someone. You can also do this when you are looking at someone's Profile.

- **Request a recommendation**: ask someone to recommend you. I will explain more in detail how to do this in a later chapter.

Account & Settings

This section is probably the least known in LinkedIn, but it really can help you to make your experience of LinkedIn much better, so take a minute to read the next few pages.

For starters you see on this screen how many introductions and InMails you still have available. You can also look at the different types of accounts.

Let's first discuss what introductions and InMails are and which account types there are available and then go more into the details of the rest of the Account & Settings page.

Introductions: messages you can send to people from your network. This means to people who are in your second or third degree. Free accounts can have 5 introductions "on the way" at the same time. Other accounts more. Remark: you can send as many messages as you want to the people from your first degree network, your direct contacts.

InMails: messages to anyone whose settings allow to accept InMails (see below for the settings). This person doesn't have to belong to your first, second or third degree. InMails are only for paid accounts.

Memberships: next to the free account there are the moment of writing 4 other memberships: Business, Business Plus, Pro and Corporate Solutions (the last one is apparently especially made for recruiters). The main difference between the paid accounts and the free account is more Introductions and InMails and the option to be part of the OpenLink network. Members of the OpenLink network can send each other messages "free" (meaning they are not taken into account in the Introductions and InMails). More information about the differences between the memberships and my opinion about them can be found in the chapter "Hot Discussion Topics and

Burning Questions". By the way, in the FAQ pages LinkedIn says, "Joining LinkedIn is and will remain free." (answer ID 55).

Now let's go through all the other options on the Account & Settings page and what they mean.

Profile Settings

Here you control your Profile. Most of the options are the same as in the "Profile" function in the left hand menu on every page, which will be covered more in detail in the next chapter.

- **My Profile**: same as "Profile" function in the left hand menu on every page

- **My Profile Photo** (also via your Profile):

  - Upload a picture

  - Make the picture available to only your own connections, your network (till third degree) or everyone

- **Public Profile**: same as under "Profile" function in the left hand menu on every page and then Edit Public Profile Settings

- **Manage Recommendations**: same as under "Profile" function in the left hand menu on every page

- **Status Visibility**: make your status visible to only your own connections, your network (till third degree) or everyone. "Status" means a description of what you are doing right now. This works like the tweets of Twitter (www.twitter.com) or the "What are you doing right now?" function of Facebook (www.facebook.com).

Email notifications

Here you control the type and amount of LinkedIn related messages and emails you receive.

- **Contact settings**:

  - *What type of messages do you want to receive*: Introductions and Inmails or Introductions only. This means you can choose between receiving only messages from people from your second and third degree (via your first degree) or also from people who are outside your network, but have a paid membership. This option can be combined with "Invitation Filtering" (see below) to only allow messages and invitations from people you know.

- *Opportunity preferences*: you can choose whether or not people can contact you for one of more of these topics:

    - Career opportunities

    - Consulting offers

    - New ventures

    - Job inquiries

    - Expertise requests

    - Business deals

    - Personal reference requests

    - Requests to reconnect

- *What advice would you give to users considering contacting you*: free text. Although I don't think many people will read this, it is a good idea to answer this question so you can refer back to that when people contact you. For example when someone contacts you via a LinkedIn message for a new job while you have written that you are only interested in Consulting Offers and only want to be contacted via email or the telephone.

- **Receiving Messages**: this is the place where you control the emails you receive from LinkedIn. The 4 options are:

    - Individual Email: Send emails to me immediately

    - Daily Digest Email: Send one bundle per day

    - Weekly Digest Email: Send one bundle email per week

    - No Email: Read messages on the website

    Some of these options are only available for individual contacts like invitations and not for Group messages and the other way around. For me the "Individual Email" option works for individual contacts and "Weekly Digest Email" for Groups works the best.

- **Invitation Filtering**: there are three options:

    o   All invitations (default)

    o   Only invitations from people who know my email address or appear in my "Imported Contacts" list.

    o   Only invitations from people who appear in my "Imported Contacts" list.

    If you get too many unwanted invitations you might consider changing your preferences here, but on the other hand you might miss many opportunities.

Home Page Settings

At the moment of writing there is only one option: the way your network updates are displayed on your Home Page.

You can decide how many updates that you want to show on your Home Page (default 15, but you can go up to 25) and which kind of updates are shown and which are hidden. For example, I'm personally interested in Questions from my connections, but not in Jobs posted by my connections (although I could use that information to help someone from my network to get a new job and someone else to get a position filled).

RSS Settings

RSS means Really Simple Syndication. What it means in practice that you can "subscribe" to information you find interesting and have it shown in an RSS reader. An RSS reader can be a webpage where all the information you subscribed to is presented to you in one overview or can be some extra folders in your email program. What RSS does in practice is present to you information you are interested in in one spot so you don't have to visit tons of websites to find it.

Here you can subscribe to the RSS feed for your personal Network Updates and Answers. By the way, each Answers category has its own feed.

If you use RSS, this might be an interesting alternative for the updates on the Home Page. Most people are more triggered by an RSS message than by the messages on their LinkedIn Home Page.

Personal Information

Here you control your basic account details.

- **Name and Location**: change your name and location. You can decide to only show the first letter of your last name for people who don't belong to your network (your network still can see your first and last name).

- **Email addresses**: add all email addresses you expect to receive invitations from. Make sure you have at least one personal address (like a Hotmail or Gmail address) that you will always keep no matter what organization you work for.

- **Change Password**: pretty obvious ☺

- **Close Your Account**: in my opinion the only reason to close a LinkedIn account is because you have more than one account. I meet many people who have opened an account three years ago when they were invited by someone and then after changing jobs opened another account. Good to know is that LinkedIn is not able to merge accounts. They advise to move all information and connections to one account and then close the other one. If you need more help with this, their help desk is there to assist you.

Privacy Settings

Here you control more of what people see from you.

- **Partner Sites**: at the moment of writing there is only one partner website (NY Times) which gives LinkedIn users a more personalized experience when surfing on the NY Times website. You can turn this option on (default) or off.

- **Research Surveys**: from the website: *"LinkedIn and its research partners may invite a select group of users to participate in online market research studies. Users are identified based on non-personal information such as job title, company size, or region. Participation is 100% voluntary and personal information such as name and email address will never be revealed."* You can choose to receive requests to participate in Online Market Research Studies that are relevant to your professional expertise (default) or not.

- **Connections Browse**: you can choose to allow people from your first degree network to see your connections (default) or not. This is an option that many times raises some discussion. See the chapter "Hot Discussion Topics and Burning Questions."

- **Profile Views**: choose what other people see when you have visited their Profile

- o Show my name and headline

- o Only show my anonymous Profile characteristics, such as industry and title (default). Remark: this is the reason why most of the times you don't see a name when using the function "Who viewed my Profile".

- o Don't show users that I've viewed their Profile

- **Viewing Profile Photos**: you can control whose Profile pictures you can see.

  - o No One
  - o My Connections
  - o My Network
  - o Everyone

    The only reason I can think of why you wouldn't choose Everyone is when you are a recruiter and you don't want to be biased.

- **Profile and Status Updates**: you can choose whether your connections are notified when you change your Profile or change your status (default) or not. "Status" is what you have filled in "What are you doing now?"

- **Service Provider Directory**: choose if you want to be listed in the Service Provider Directory (default) or not. To be actually listed you need at least one Recommendation.

- **Authorized Applications**: at the moment of writing there were no applications available yet.

My Network

At the moment of writing there was only one option: Using Your Network. Here you can choose how your network can help you (none or all can be selected):

- Find a job
- Find consulting or contracting positions
- Hire employees or contractors
- Sell products or services to companies

- Investigate deals with companies

- Find information about industries, products, or companies

- Find professionals interested in my new venture or product

Conclusion of this chapter

By now you must have a feeling of the functionality the LinkedIn website offers. You have also received some extra information about what some of the options mean and how they can help you to use LinkedIn more effectively and efficiently.

Now let's see in the next chapter how we can actually start using LinkedIn in a way that brings results.

How To Use LinkedIn: Basic Strategy

In this chapter we will go through a basic strategy to be successful at LinkedIn. This basic strategy is for everyone. In a next chapter we will focus on more advanced strategies geared to the different "tasks" we have discussed in the first chapter.

In this chapter we will focus on making a good Profile, how to build your network, how to make connections, how to build your visibility and what the added value of Groups is.

Although I have already mentioned that it is best to be logged in to LinkedIn while reading this book, this is especially true for this chapter.

Crafting a Good Profile

To be found by other people starts with having a good Profile. Also if you send invitations to other people your Profile is very important for others to decide whether or not they are going to connect with you.

Having a Profile, which contains the right information also, allows you to increase your visibility, which supports your personal branding and online reputation. This will make it easier to attract the right people to you.

It is also very important to know that a good Profile not only increases your visibility on LinkedIn, but also on the web. Google and other search engines also index part of the information on LinkedIn: from your Public Profile. Since LinkedIn has a large PageRank in Google (which means that LinkedIn is a very popular website) the Profiles will also appear very high in search results.

One remark before we start: some people have the tendency to look at their Profile from another point of view than it really happened (yes, I mean they lie ☺). Avoid doing that, people will find out and it will always be at the worst moment in time.

As a general rule: LinkedIn is a business networking website. The focus is on the business side of people (with also a small part for personal interests). More and more people use LinkedIn to look someone up before they have a meeting with them. This means that LinkedIn is the first professional impression someone has of you. So make your first impression a good one!

Let's look at what you can do to increase your Profile on LinkedIn and on the web.

1. **Your Name, Professional Headline, Location and Industry**:

   - **Name** if you want to be found by other people who know you, use the name you use in a professional environment. So no nick names.

   - **Professional Headline:** describe your current function. If you want to be found by others on LinkedIn and on the web, use words that other people use to search people with a function like yours. If the title on your business card is Marcom Director, but people search with Vice President Marketing or Communication Manager, chances are small that you will be found.

     The headline is very important because this is the first thing that people see when they do a search and what is shown when you answer a question in Answers or in a Discussion. In many cases the Headline will encourage or discourage people to click on your name to read your Profile.

   - **Location:** Although you have to fill in your postal code, this is not shared with others on LinkedIn. For privacy reasons LinkedIn works with geographic areas instead of exact addresses.

   - **Primary industry of expertise**: fill this one to find colleagues in other companies in your industry and to be found by them. If your industry is missing in the list LinkedIn provides you with, you can suggest one.

2. **Your Profile Photo**: use a professional picture. Especially students tend to put holiday pictures on their LinkedIn Profile like they would do on Facebook. Since LinkedIn is a professional website it is better to have a "normal" picture. By the way, since there is not much space for your picture, just your head will be enough. Although it is not necessary to upload a picture, this makes it easier for others to remember you. For people who have never met you, a picture might give them more confidence that you are serious about networking on LinkedIn. So I would suggest that you upload a picture and make it visible for everybody who visits your Profile.

3. **Your Status**: tell other people what you are doing. This is comparable to Twitter or "What are you doing?" on Facebook or other websites. You have 100 characters for the text. This is also called microblogging.
   If you fill something in other members of LinkedIn will be notified, depending on your own "Profile and Update settings" in the "Privacy Settings" part of the "Account & Settings" page. It also depends on

whether the people you allow to see these updates have included these updates on their "Home Page" settings on their "Account & Settings" page.

4. **Public Profile**:

   - **Your Public Profile URL**: personalize your LinkedIn Profile page by using your name in the URL. This will boost your online presence on the web: when someone searches on your name in Google, Yahoo, MSN Live Search or another search engine your LinkedIn page will be in the top rankings. The URL's are unique so be the first to have a LinkedIn URL with your name.

   - You can also choose which details of your Profile are visible to people who are not logged in to LinkedIn. This means: when someone does a search on the web with your name and finds your LinkedIn page, which details do you allow them to see?

5. **Summary**:

   - **Professional Experience and Goals**: free text. If you write more than two lines, make it more pleasant to the eye to read it. Use, for example, bullets or dashes. Also don't put too much text here because people won't read it. Focus on the results you have obtained, not on the task you did. This will appeal much more to the reader.
   This is also a good spot to share what you can offer people without expecting anything in return. For example, in my Profile I share that the visitor of my Profile can subscribe to a free networking e-course on the website of Networking Coach (www.networking-coach.com)
   If you talk about yourself, use "I" and not "He" or "She". The latter puts people off. You don't talk about yourself in the "He" or "She" form when you have a normal conversation with someone. Think of your Profile as a "virtual you" who responds on your behalf to the questions "What do you do? What is your expertise? What do you have to offer?" when someone visits the page.

   - **Specialties in Your Industries of Expertise**: this is the place to share the skills and knowledge you have accumulated in all the jobs you have done. This is the place to share what your expertise is. If you have a certification like Microsoft Certified Systems Engineer, this is the place to mention it. Also use the abbreviation if it is used a lot. In this example that would be MCSE.

6. **Experience**: here you can list all the organizations you have worked for. Always be sure to add a title and the right time period. This will help other people to find you and it will help you to find old colleagues back. Make sure you fill this in because we are going to need it to build your network. It is also a good idea to add one or more specific results for this work experience if you haven't done this in the summary.

7. **Education**: list the schools you went to in order to find old classmates and people who went to the same school. Even if there is 10 years in between, having studied at the same school or university or having belonged to the same student union, creates an instant bond between two people. Depending on their experiences this might be a weak or a strong bond, but it is something you have in common which makes conversations online and offline easier. Make sure you fill this in because we are going to need it to build your network.

8. **Additional information**:

   • **Websites**: visibility tip: use the "other" option and then give your own description. Why? Because this helps for the search engine rankings of your own websites. Search engine rankings take into account links from other websites (in this case LinkedIn), the PageRank of these websites (in the case of LinkedIn it is 8 which is very high) and also the words that are used in the description. For example, instead of using "My Company" I have used "Other" in my Profile. Then I put in the name Networking Coach and the URL www.networking-coach.com. When someone searches in Google with the words networking coach this small tweak in LinkedIn will help to get a higher ranking (actually this is one of the techniques that allowed us to be number one in Google worldwide for the words networking coach).

   • **Interests**: list some of your personal interests here. Next to the professional information that is already abundantly present in your Profile personal interests and hobbies help other people to get a better image of you as a whole person. Many times common interests are found in this small box, which make online and offline conversations much easier.

   • **Groups and Associations**: list here which groups and associations you belong to. Don't confuse this with the Groups on LinkedIn. List here all the associations and clubs you are a member of outside LinkedIn. Of course some of these organizations will also have an online presence on LinkedIn, but the LinkedIn Groups you belong to are automatically added to your Profile.

- **Honors and awards**: if you have received awards or honors that are relevant for your Profile, list them here. If they help other people to have a better picture of who you are as a person or which expertise you have, list them. Otherwise it is better not to mention them because it might confuse people.

9. **Contact settings**: this is a link to this item on the Account & Settings page.

10. **Applications**: you can choose to add some applications to your Profile like your blog or a Slideshare presentation.

One general tip for all fields: if you want to be found on LinkedIn, use the words people will use when they look for your expertise or the things you might have in common. Use synonyms (for example, Marketing Manager in your title and Marketing Director in the description) and both abbreviations and full names (for example, UCLA and University of California, Los Angeles).

If you are not sure what exactly to write down: LinkedIn offers examples for most parts of the Profile. It is also a good idea to look at other people's Profiles. Use the ones you like the best as a model for your own. It is also always a good idea to ask someone else's opinion about your Profile. Some things are so obvious to us that we forget to mention them or we don't see them as skills or strengths. Other people might help you to look at it more objectively.

An extra tip is to use the Google Keyword tool to find more synonyms or suggestion for alternative words. This tool is primarily used for Google ads, but you can also use it to find the right words for your Profile. This free tool can be found at: https://adwords.google.com/select/KeywordToolExternal (or use search on "Google Keyword Tool"). One remark: don't overdo it. Don't stuff your Profile with keywords. People still need to be able to read it.

How to build your network ... Fast

In my network book, "Let's Connect!" I wrote about the 6 degrees of proximity (better known as the theory of the 6 degrees of separation): we live indeed in a small world. LinkedIn helps us to discover these links by presenting us ALL the mutual contacts and is hence a super powerful tool.

The only disadvantage is that LinkedIn only shows the network till the third degree. Fourth degrees and further are not in your LinkedIn network anymore.

To really benefit from the enormous power of LinkedIn it is necessary to build our own first degree network. The real power of the network is in the second degree, but to be able to reach second and third degrees we need first degree contacts first.

So let's look at a strategy on how to build a network on LinkedIn. And moreover how we can build it fast.

Phase 1: Lay the Foundation of your Network

1. **Upload your contacts from Outlook, webmail like Hotmail, Gmail, Yahoo or AOL or other address books.** You can do this via the green "Add Connections" button in the menu on the left on every page and then click on the "Import Contact" tab.
    When you upload these contacts they are only visible to you. There is also no message sent by LinkedIn.

    Remark: this is what you need to do when you get a processing error when you use Vista and Internet Explorer 7 (from the LinkedIn Help pages):

    Security settings on Internet Explorer 7 running on Windows Vista may cause you to receive the following error: 'There was an error processing your request'. To upload your contacts you will need to modify your Security settings.

    - *Open Internet Explorer 7.*

    - *Go to 'Tools' and choose 'Internet Options'.*

    - *Select the 'Security' tab.*

    - *Select the 'Internet' zone.*

    - *Disable/uncheck the checkbox called 'Enable Protected Mode'.*

    - *Click 'Apply', then 'OK' until you exit this dialog.*

    - *Restart IE 7 - The status bar at the bottom should now state 'Internet | Protected Mode: Off'.*

    - *Retry uploading your contacts to LinkedIn.*

2. **Look at the contacts, which are now available in "Imported Contacts"** (under "Contacts" in the menu on the left on every page). The people who are already on LinkedIn have a small blue icon with the letters "In". Since they are already using LinkedIn they will be open for a connection with you.

   Select the people who are already on LinkedIn and who you know (with some people you may have just exchanged business cards with them10 years ago which decreases the chance that they will remember you and you them in some cases). If you have lots of people in your address book this might take a while and several pages to go through. If this is the case for you, you can divide this group in several smaller ones. The people you have selected will appear on the right hand side.

3. **Write a semi-personal message to them**. First check "Add a personal note to your invitation". Then replace the standard "Hi, I'd like to add you to my network" message with a semi-personal one. You can't make it too personal when you use this method because you have selected several people. To give you an idea what this might look like, this is an example of a message that I used recently:

   > *I see you are a member of LinkedIn as well.*
   >
   > *Let's Connect! :-)*
   >
   > *By the way did you know that the "Group" functionality has improved a lot with the "Discussions"?*
   >
   > *In the meanwhile there are already many Groups in different sectors and professions.*
   >
   > *It's definitely worth your while to find out which Groups are interesting to you.*
   >
   > *Have a great networking day!*
   >
   > *Jan*

   A few remarks:

   - **You don't see any name at the beginning of the message**. The reason is that LinkedIn automatically adds the first name of the person to the message. Since there is no preview function, this is something that only a few people know!

   - You see that my **message in itself is not personal, but I make it less a mass mail by adding a tip**. I got many good reactions after connecting with people using this message. Many people told me they hadn't really looked into the Groups functionality. This tip doesn't have to be related to LinkedIn. If you connect with people with the same function you might share a trend or the link to an interesting article. It doesn't have to be much, but the recipient must perceive it as valuable (more tips about what you can offer to other people can be found in my book, "Let's Connect!"). Always add something extra to the invitations you send to people. Remember, this is an extra contact moment with someone. The better you do this, the faster you can get results. People who have received the invitation with the tip might remember you and might get back in touch with you to see if you can work together in one way or the other.

- If you have a large address book you want to split it into more groups. At the same time **you don't want to type your message again and again**. Of course, you can use notepad or Word to store your text and do copy/paste. However, there is also another tool that you can use for many repeating tasks, which can help you with this. It is called "Texter". Read more in the chapter "Free Tools to save you time when working with LinkedIn".

After doing these 3 steps people will respond to you. They will accept your invitation and your network will start to grow.

Phase 2: A Second Layer for your Network.

While you are waiting for people to accept the invitations you have sent in phase 1, you can add more people to your network. Again we first focus on the people who are already on LinkedIn because they will be more open to accept your invitation.

We will use the tools LinkedIn provides for retrieving colleagues and classmates. Since LinkedIn works with the information in your Profile it is important that you have filled in the companies you have worked for and the schools and universities you went to.

Let's start with current and past colleagues.

1. **Look for current and past colleagues.** You can do this via the green "Add Connections" button in the menu on the left on every page and then click on the "Colleagues" tab.
   You will see all the companies that you have listed yourself in your Profile. You will also see how many people from each company are already LinkedIn members.

2. **Click on a company** you are working for or have worked for. You will get a list of people you might know. Select the people you actually know.

3. Write a **personal message** to them if you are going to invite them one by one or write a **semi-personal message** like the one in step 3 of phase 1.

4. Repeat steps 2 and 3 for every company.

In this way your network grows with current and past colleagues.

Now we are going to do the same for the people you studied with (or are studying with). While you might have fewer contacts or current interests on a professional or personal level with them, old classmates might be very valuable for your network. Remember the fundamental principle of the weak ties and the importance of a diverse network.

1. **Look for classmates.** You can do this via the green "Add Connections" button in the menu on the left on every page and then click on the "Classmates" tab.
    You will see all the schools that you have listed yourself in your Profile.

2. **Click on a school**. You will get a list of people you might know. Select the people you actually know. You can only select one classmate at the time.

3. Write a **personal message** to them.

4. Repeat steps 2 and 3 for every classmate of that same school.

5. Repeat steps 2, 3 and 4 for every school you studied at.

In this way your network grows with current and past classmates.

Phase 3: The Third Layer of your Network

The next step you can take is inviting people you know, but who are not on LinkedIn. Now it is very important to avoid the standard invitation message. Why? Because these people might never have heard of LinkedIn. When they get an email from the LinkedIn mail server with an impersonal message from you they might think it is SPAM and delete the message. And that's not the action you want them to take!

How do we do this?

Again we are going to use the tools LinkedIn provides.

Since you already imported your Outlook or Webmail address book in phase 1, we are going to start from there.

1. Go to the "**Imported Contacts**" under "Contacts".

2. **Select the people** you want to invite.

3. Write a **personal message** to them if you want to invite them one by one or write a **semi-personal message** if you want to invite a group of people at once.
    First check "Add a personal note to your invitation". Then replace the standard "Hi, I'd like to add you to my network" message with a personal or semi-personal one. This is an example of a semi-personal one:

    > Have you already heard of the LinkedIn website?
    > I'm now a user for a week and already was able to reconnect with people from my professional network and also with old classmates. One of the advantages of LinkedIn is that it helps to keep in touch with your network even if they change jobs or move to another country.
    >
    > I would like to invite you to also join. It is free so that is already a barrier less ☺
    >
    > Whether you join or not, drop me a message to let me know how you are doing.
    >
    > Jan

    Of course you can change this message depending on the background of the people you send this message to. For example, you can select a group of old colleagues from company ABC and refer to particular things or people in that company. It is also a good idea to change the message when you invite suppliers or customers.

    Since most standard invitation messages (and also the example I just gave you, but in a lesser extent) might feel like a sales pitch, you might also include an offer to help them set up a Profile by taking a few minutes and talking them through it via the phone.

An alternative for using the imported contacts is to invite people manually. These are the steps to take:

1. Click on the green "Add Connections" button. You will automatically land on the **"Invite Contacts"** page.

2. **Fill in the first name, last name and email address** of the people you want to invite. You can invite maximum 6 people at the same time.

3. See step 3 above.

A third way to invite people is from within Outlook.

LinkedIn provides a toolbar for Outlook that can be downloaded for free from the LinkedIn website (look at the bottom of the page). When you have installed this toolbar a small icon "Info" appears in every email. When you right-click with your mouse on this icon you have the option to invite this person if he is not in your LinkedIn network yet. Interesting fact is that this toolbar comes with a set of different invitation templates while on the website there is only one invitation message. More about this toolbar in the chapter "Free Tools to save you time when working with LinkedIn".

Phase 4: Grow your Network Passively

In the first three phases you took action to invite other people by sending them an invitation message. In phase 4 you will set up some tools that will passively invite people to connect with you, which means you set them up once and then don't have to invest time in them anymore.

1. Mention your LinkedIn Profile in your email signature. How?

   - Scroll to the bottom of a page on LinkedIn. Next to "Tools" click on "Overview".

   - In the middle of the page, you see "Email signature". Click on the "Try it now" button.

   - Create your LinkedIn email signature.

2. Mention you LinkedIn Profile on your website or blog.

   - Click on "Edit Profile" in the left hand menu

   - Click on "Edit Public Profile Settings" on top at the right hand side

   - Click on "Promote your Profile with customized buttons" (approximately 4th line, this one is hidden well)

- Choose the button and code you want to use on your website or blog.

When you are going to use these email signatures and buttons some people will click on it and invite you to connect with them. In this way THEY take action not you, that's why I call phase 4 a passive phase.

By going through the first 3 phases you will lay the foundation of your network. Over time phase 4 will bring you more connections.

One of the mistakes I see people make the most in networking is that they only start to build their network when they need it: when they are looking for a new job or when they need new customers. The danger of doing that is that you will definitely need some time to build your network and you may not have this time. An even greater danger is that you will contact people out of a need. In such a situation it is hard to network without expecting something immediately in return. People will feel that. As a consequence, many will be reluctant to connect with you and make introductions for you.

So avoid that situation and start building your network right now!

In a next chapter you will get some extra advanced strategies for further expanding your network. Start now to build the foundation of your network.

What you will experience is that your network will expand automatically. Other LinkedIn members will find you and invite you to connect with them. People from your network will also discover LinkedIn, become a member and then invite you to connect. Another interesting fact is that the larger your network grows, the more people will be interested in connecting with you. Even people you don't know. How to deal with them will be discussed in the chapter "Hot Discussion Topics and Burning Questions".

The Added Value of Groups

As I already mentioned in the introduction of this book, the trigger that caused me to actually write this book is the Group functionality that has improved a lot the last few months.

Why is that?

Before the Discussions function was added to the Groups, LinkedIn was primarily a directory of people with the links between them. The Answers functionality brought more interaction on the website, but since the introduction of the Discussions function LinkedIn is going towards a real community where people can help each other and receive help from each other.

The building of relationships resides in the actions between the members, not in the fact that their Profiles are linked to each other. Discussions and the sharing of News makes this not only lots easier, but it gives the opportunity to tap into the power of Groups: 2 know more than 1, 3 more than 2 and so on.

Become a member

Interactions in Groups are also more intuitive than the Answers functionality. People are used to coming together in clubs and associations in real life. Sharing ideas is also one of the first things the Internet was used for.

So I encourage you to become a member of one or more Groups or start one yourself. Once you are member these are the benefits of belonging to one:

- By asking questions in the Discussions-forum you are able to **receive help from the other members**.

- **You can see the Profiles of the other members**. This gives you direct access to additional people who might not be in your first, second or third degree network.

- **You can contact other members directly**. Many people don't allow to be contacted directly (they disable that option in their Account & Settings). However, the standard option in every Group is that members can contact each other directly. Almost nobody knows this option can be turned off.

- **By answering questions in the Discussions-forum you not only gain visibility, but you also have the opportunity to show your expertise**. As a consequence, your "Know, Like and Trust" factor increases. When you answer questions, make sure you give good answers and don't make it a sales pitch.

- **By sharing articles in News you also raise your visibility**. Again don't make it a sales pitch. It is OK to share links to your own website, blog or article that features you as long as it gives other people more insights or helps them in some way.

- **When responding to a question in the Discussions you can add the URL of your website**. This gives your website more visibility and helps to boost your ranking in Google and other search engines. However, don't overdo it. One, maximum two lines.

- **Some extra advantages of being a member of a Group which also organizes meetings where the members can meet each other face to face**:

- You can ask who else is going so you can make a decision if it is worthwhile for you. You can also make arrangements to meet other people there. This helps a lot when you are not comfortable in new environments.

- If you have never been to a meeting, you can ask about the past experiences of other members and which expectations you can have

- You can make arrangements to car pool so you don't only save some money and are friendly to the environment, but also can maximize your networking time.

- Tips about how to prepare for live networking events, what to do when you are there and how to follow up, can be found on the networking CD, "Let's Connect at an Event".

I strongly encourage you to become a member of one or more Groups. I also encourage you to be an active member: help people and share insights. This will make you more attractive for other people. They will make contact with you and consult you in your area of expertise, whatever that may be.

The biggest question for many people remains: which Groups do I have to join? In the next chapter with Advanced Strategies I will go deeper into detail because it depends on your Profile.

For now I can share these tips because they apply to everybody:

- Alumnl groups of schools (former students)
- Alumnl groups of companies (former employees and many times also current employees)
- Groups of the organization you work for
- Groups of organizations you belong to in the real world

How to find a Group on LinkedIn?

1. In the left hand menu, click "Groups"

2. Then click on the menu item "Groups Directory" (at the top of the new page) or click on the right hand side on the button "Find a Group".

3. Then use the search box in the new button. You can refine your search with the type of Group you are looking for or the language.

Some people browse rather than search. LinkedIn doesn't offer that function. An alternative is the list that Jacco Valkenburg, author of "Recruitment via LinkedIn", offers on his website http://www.recruitmentvialinkedin.com

Note: when joining Groups keep in mind that you can be a member of a maximum of 50 Groups.

Become a Group Manager

And why not create your own Group? As a Group owner you have a special status, which raises your visibility. However, do this only if you have enough time to spend on managing a Group. This means inviting people to the Group, accepting Join Requests and most importantly keeping the conversation going. You have to post questions and answers to questions. Although this might scare you, there is also good news: you don't have to do this alone. Up to 10 people can be the manager of a Group.

See the chapter for Advanced Strategies for Organizers and Group Managers for many more tips.

Maintaining Relationships

LinkedIn is not only a great tool to find people, but also to maintain your relationships. These are some actions you might take on LinkedIn (next to the many other things you can do via email, telephone or when you meet them):

- Introduce two of your LinkedIn contacts to each other. By far the best networking action you can do. It doesn't cost you any money and just a very small amount of time. The results for your contacts might be huge.

- Write a Recommendation for your contacts.

- Suggest one of your contacts as an expert in Answers.

- Refer to one of your contacts as an expert in a Discussion in one of your LinkedIn Groups.

- Suggest interesting LinkedIn Groups to your contacts.

- Notify your contacts when there is a question (in Answers or in a Discussion) in their area of expertise.

- Notify your contacts of interesting events that are posted on LinkedIn or somewhere else. By posting this in a Discussion in a Group you can notify more people at once and increase your own visibility.

- When you see in the Updates that someone got promoted or changed position, this is a good trigger to congratulate her.

Note: a feature that is at the time of writing still in beta phase is the notes in the Profiles of your first degree connections. When you are looking at someone's Profile, scroll down and at the right hand side you will see a box titled "Your private info about *name*". You can add some notes here or click below on "Add/view contact details" and add some more details. In other words, LinkedIn is adding some CRM (Contact Relationship Management) functionality here.

I'm not inclined to transfer all the contact details and extra information I have to LinkedIn and only rely on LinkedIn as my contact system. Why? Because your contacts might delete their Profile or disconnect from you. And then you lose all your information.

Raising your Visibility and Credibility with Answers

I just explained that the value of the Groups functionality is in the interactions between people. Before the Discussions function was introduced, there was already another tool that stimulated interaction: the Answers.

Actually the concept is pretty simple. Some people ask questions and others answer them.

Again this allows you to receive help from the network on the one hand and raise your visibility and credibility on the other hand.

Just by answering questions you will be on other people's radar.

When responding to a question you can also add the URL of your website. This gives your website more visibility and helps to boost your ranking in Google and other search engines. However, don't overdo it. One, maximum two lines.

If they really think you are an expert in your field of expertise, they will give you expert points. These points are awarded by the person asking a question to the person they thought gave the best answer.

Once you have gained some expert points you will also be listed in the experts directory, which raises your Profile even more. How many points you need to be in that list depends on the category. In some categories there are only few questions and also only a few people who answer them. It is easier to get in the expert list of that category. But since there are not so many questions your visibility as an expert will be limited.

Does that mean you shouldn't put in any effort? No, it is not about the expert points, but about genuinely helping other people and sharing good tips. By doing this you will be perceived as an expert.

However, since the categories are open for everybody and worldwide, this might not be the place you want to focus your attention and time on. Answering questions in the Groups that you have chosen gives you much faster visibility and more credibility. However, in Groups you can't earn expert points (you won't get expert points in private messages, only in public ones).

The advantage of Answers on the other hand is that all the answers are stored and visible for everybody months after you have answered a question. So this is another way of passively raising your visibility and credibility. Answers in Groups are not searchable and can only be browsed by people who are a member of that Group.

Note: if you ask a question yourself whether in Answers or in a Group, people appreciate knowing what you did with the input you got. So take the time to react.

Conclusion of this chapter

In this chapter you have gone through a basic strategy so you know how to use LinkedIn and to make LinkedIn work for you.

After you crafted your profile you have built your network in 4 phases: importing your contacts, contacting current and old colleagues and classmates, inviting your contacts who are not a LinkedIn member yet and making a LinkedIn signature or banner.

Then you learned the added value of Groups both as a member and Group Manager, how to maintain relationships using LinkedIn and how to raise your visibility and credibility using Answers.

Now let's turn to the next chapter to understand more deeply how to tap into the power of our network and how to use LinkedIn as the tool to accomplish that. This will be the foundation for the advanced strategies.

Experience the Power of LinkedIn

One of the most frequently asked questions in our networking and referral training courses is: "Which groups, associations and organizations do I have to be a member of?" and also "Where do I start with networking? How can I tap into the power of my network?"

Most of us grow our online and offline networks rather accidentally: we start working for a certain employer and meet colleagues, customers, suppliers and partners. We go to a conference and meet other participants. We attend a seminar or training course and meet new people. We become a member of an organization and meet other members.

Most of these encounters between people are rather random and are a consequence of being at the same spot or in the same situation. This is important in networking, especially to get new ideas and new perspectives.

On the other hand many people complain about the lack of a work-life balance. They tell us they can't spend another evening from home to attend another reception, conference or another networking event. Or they tell us that they actually don't have time to join LinkedIn or other networking websites. But they still do because other people tell them they have to do it or share success stories. However, they only feel like it is a waste of their time.

When I ask them "When attending a networking event or joining a Group on LinkedIn, how does that relate to your goals?" almost all of them remain silent. Why? Because they have never REALLY given thought to their goals.

And that is the clue to successful networking: starting from your goals and then making decisions which online and offline groups and associations to join.

For some people this approach might seem very goal oriented which takes the fun and spontaneity out of the interactions between people.

At first sight that might be the case, but actually starting from your goals will allow you to be more spontaneous to other people. Since you know who might help you, you can lower your expectations of your conversations with all other people. This gives more room for spontaneous conversations.

This chapter is divided in three segments. First we are going to do the GAIN exercise as a preparation for the second and third segment. In that second segment you will receive insights in the one super tool that leverages LinkedIn, the Magic Email. In the third part you will experience where the real power of LinkedIn resides.

G.A.I.N. exercise

G.A.I.N. is the abbreviation for

Goal

Achieving via the

Immense Power of your

Network.

In this exercise you will lay the foundation of your advanced strategies on LinkedIn. This exercise will only take 10 minutes and is the only exercise in the book. If you are like me, you will want to skip the exercise and read on. However, I really suggest you do this exercise. It will help you much better to understand and experience how the power of networking can be taken to the next level using LinkedIn.

3 Step Process

The GAIN method consists of an exercise in 2 or 3 steps:

1. The first step is setting a goal.
2. In the second step we are going to look at who are the people in the best position to help you reach this goal.
3. The third (and optional) step is to compare notes and exchange ideas with other people who also did the first two steps. This helps to generate new ideas and many times they can make some connections for you and vice versa.

Let's look at the three steps in detail.

Step 1: Set a Goal

Before we start, I want to share with you my own ideas about goals. Someone once said: "A goal is a dream with a deadline." That is a good start when thinking about goals and how to reach them. I make the distinction about big goals and sub goals.

Let me give you a personal example. A few years ago I wanted to write a book and make it number 1 on Amazon. These are already two goals, not one. Number one is writing a book and number two is getting it on the number 1 position on Amazon.

Now for many people both goals look like an enormous challenge, like a mountain that is too big and steep to climb. As a consequence, they never start.

So what did I do? For starters I separated the two goals. Then I made sub goals: I wasn't going to write the book at once, but chapter after chapter, subchapter after subchapter. If you have projects of 10 pages it is easier than a project of 250 pages. Then I added some extra sub goals for getting the book published: find out how a book gets into a bookstore, how to get an ISBN number, how to get a photographer for my picture on the back,... And I did the same for getting the book at number 1.

So I made sub goals and sub-sub goals: these are small projects that are not that difficult to do and don't take that much time.

Maybe you are wondering now: what was the result? Did you write the book? And did it reach number 1 on Amazon?

Yes, I wrote "Let's Connect!" and no, it didn't reach the overall number 1 position on Amazon. But it did reach the number 2 position for marketing books, making me the first Belgian author to achieve that position.

Am I disappointed? No! If someone had told me before I started writing, "Let's Connect!" that it would be the number 2 marketing book on Amazon, I would never have believed them.

So what I want to share with you is: make goals and make them big. There is a saying "Shoot for the moon, if you miss you will land among the stars." Many people have dreams and goals in their heads, but they think they will never be able to reach them. What happens next? Nothing. They just keep doing what they have been doing and nothing changes. Reaching your goals starts with writing them down, even if they seem unattainable to you. I shot for the moon (number 1 position on Amazon) and landed among the stars (number 2 marketing book). If I hadn't set the goal of being overall number one, there wouldn't have been a number 2 spot for marketing books either.

Maybe you also heard that in goal setting your goal needs to be SMART. I would like to invite you to make your goals SMARTER. SMARTER is an acronym and means:

- **S**pecific
- **M**easurable
- **A**ction-oriented
- **R**ealistic

- **T**imely
- **E**thical
- **R**egistered

Let's look at what each of those words mean.

- **S**pecific: the more concrete the better. Numbers make goals more specific and more concrete. Also think about geography or language if that is relevant for your goal.

- **M**easurable: numbers and dates make your goal more measurable.

- **A**ction-oriented: use a verb. And use a verb that you are familiar with what it means in practice. For example: a nurse probably doesn't know all actions that are linked to the word "sell" and a sales person probably doesn't know all the actions of nursing (and how to do them).

- **R**ealistic: make your goals challenging and attainable at the same time. That's why some goals need sub goals. The big goal doesn't seem realistic or attainable at all, but the sub goals might be rather easy to achieve.

- **T**imely: put a date or a timeframe on your goal. Again it might be easier when you divide a larger goal into smaller ones. It is easier to put a time estimate on a small project than on a big one. Smaller goals are easier and faster to achieve. Achieving small goals is also more motivating to keep going.

- **E**thical: the goal can't harm others. So think and feel whether your goal is ethical on all levels. Change it when necessary.

- **R**egistered: write your goal down. Many people have their dreams and goals in their head. The first step to achieve them is to write them down.

I also want to add two extra elements:

- **The goal needs to inspire you and motivate you.** For me picturing the idea of having my book on Amazon gave me enough drive to keep working on the goal. Sometimes a participant in a presentation says, "I want to be the president of the United States". When I ask them a few questions it is clear that it is just a joke and even more, the real vision of being the president with many responsibilities doesn't inspire or motivate them at all.

- **It has to be your goal and not someone else's.** This is linked to the previous remark. If someone else gives you a goal you won't be very motivated most of the time. You probably will work on it, but never have the drive to really go for it and to go the extra mile (or extra hours) to achieve it. Don't get me wrong, you don't have to work long hours to reach your goals. What I want to say is that if it is your own goal that really motivates you, it won't feel like work or a burden. On the contrary you can't wait to work on it. That's why I'm a big advocate of joint goal setting by managers and their team members so team members can set their own goals that are related to the bigger ones of the organization.

Your first assignment now is to write down one goal. This could be to find a new job, to increase sales, to find partners to work together with,... Make it as SMARTER as possible. For the sake of the exercise take a goal you want to achieve within 1 year maximum. Divide your goal in sub goals when necessary.

For example: let's assume your goal is to increase sales by 10% in the next year. What does that mean? How many customers are we talking about? If you have more than one product: how many new or repeat customers do you need for each of them? In which region or country do you want to have those sales? By replacing percentages with absolute numbers it becomes clearer whether the goal is realistic or not.

Write down one goal now.

_____

_____

_____

_____

Look at your goal again. Is it SMARTER? Take an especially good look at the S (specific). From the thousands of people who have done this exercise before you in our training courses or presentations most of them didn't make their goal specific enough.

Why is that so important? If your goal is not specific enough, it will be harder for you to take action. The second reason is that it will also be harder for other people to see how they can help you. And then you can't tap into the power of networking.

Step 2: People in the Best Position to Help You

After setting your goal, the next step is defining who the people are who are in the best position to help you reach your goal.

Assignment: fill in the next table the first 5 rows (not all 8 yet, we'll come back to the remaining 3 later) with the 5 people who are in the best position to help you reach your goal.

Nr	Person	Added value (why do you choose this person and not someone else)	What can you do for this person?
1			
2			
3			
4			
5			
6			
7			
8			

After you have filled in the first 5 rows, here are some tips to look at this table from a different point of view and to get some new ideas.

1. **Have you only written down people you already know**? Or have you really written the people in the best position? When we do this exercise with groups, many people translate the assignment in their brains. Instead of hearing "Write down the people who are in the best position to help you reach your goal" they hear "Write down the people YOU KNOW who are in the best position to help you reach your goal". This is one of most limiting factors people have in networking: they limit themselves to the people they know. So think now who are **really the people in the best position to help you reach your goal** even if you don't know them yet. If you don't know their name, just write down a function or a description.

2. Another category, which might be useful, is **mentors, coaches or people who could be a soundboard for you**. They might not be able to help you with the goal itself, but they can be of great help on the way towards the goal. For example, they can check whether your goal is SMARTER and ask questions about the results you have achieved up till now. You can pay for a coach, but your colleague, spouse, neighbor or aunt can also be good soundboards.

3. A third category of people is people who **have a large network and who are willing to make introductions for you.** We call these people "connectors." Via these connectors you can reach many people.

4. A last tip to further fill in the table is investigating the second column. What have you written down there? Which information, connections, knowledge or other information does this person have which make him an added value for your goal? Now think who else (who is not on your list yet **can deliver the same value**? This is a way of reverse thinking to get some extra ideas.

Remark: most people have a hard time to fill in the third column. You don't have to do something for someone else. People like to help each other, especially when it doesn't cost any money and only a small part of their time (that's why it is so important to make your goals as SMARTER as possible so people can decide right away whether they can help you or not).

The reason why I added this third column is that many people don't ask for help because they have the feeling that they only take from other people. As a consequence, they have the feeling that the relationship will not be in balance anymore. By thinking up front what they might do for someone else, they might already find some "mental rest". They then realize that they are not "takers". For many people this also ensures they feel more confident to actually contact this person.

If you really don't know what you could do for the other person, but you still feel it is important, then there is still one option: ask this person. Don't do this at the beginning, but at the end of the conversation. For example, ask which project he is working on and what help he might want. Then see if you can help this person yourself or with whom from your network who has the right knowledge, experience or skills you can connect this person.

By the way, how do you ask for help? Don't beg, but ask for advice! It was Christine Comaford-Lynch in her book, "Rules for Renegades" who gave me deeper insight in what a difference it makes how you ask for help. When you share your goal and then ask for advice, it is surprising how many people will help you and give you even more information and introductions than you would ever have imagined.

Assignment: fill in the remaining rows from the table.

Now look at your table. You not only see now which people from your network can help you, but also who they are and which function they have. With this knowledge you can now make better decisions which organizations to join in real life and which Groups on LinkedIn.

You will still have some "blind spots": some people who are in the best position to help you reach your goal, but who you don't know yet. That is what we are going to use LinkedIn for.

Step 3: Tap into the Power of your Network (optional)

The third step we do in our training courses and presentations is have the participants share their goal and table from step 1 and 2 with one or more people.

This is a very interesting exercise, which works in two directions:

1. The person who explains his goal and who shares what he has written in the table often gets new ideas only by speaking about it to others aloud. Next to that he receives feedback from the other people related to his goal (is it SMARTER or not) or to the table. He often receives other approaches or new ideas from the other participants. In many cases even specific names or introductions!

2. The ones who are listening most of the time hear new ideas or other approaches which they can apply to their goal or their table.

What we often see happening when people have done this exercise in one of our sessions is that they start doing this exercise on a regular basis. For example, with colleagues during a lunch or with other business owners during a monthly meeting.

Assignment: invite 3 or 4 people to do this exercise with. This can be just once or on a regular basis.

If you decide not to do step 3 as it is presented here, it is still a good idea to share your goal and table with one person and ask for their feedback.

The Magic Email

By now you understand the power of a network and how it can help you reach your goals. I hope you now see the benefit of using LinkedIn in your strategy. The enormous power of LinkedIn lies in the fact that it makes the connections between people visible and also via whom of your network you might reach the people in the best position to help you.

Before we look at how to use LinkedIn, I want to share with you the one tool that brought in enormous results from networking for my company and for everybody who attended one of our training courses or seminars.

I call this tool the Magic Email.

What is this about? In the Magic Email you are introduced by someone you know to someone who can help you reach your goals. It is an email from someone from your first degree network to your second degree network. It is an email from someone who knows both parties.

We already talked about the "Know, Like and Trust" factor before. The more trust there is, the more inclined someone will be to help you reach your goal, hire you or become a customer. In his book, "The Speed of Trust" Stephen M.R. Covey gives many examples of how and when people trust each other so everything goes faster. One of the messages in the book is that trust can also be transferred from one person to another person.

The good news is that LinkedIn is the ultimate tool to transfer trust from one person to another if used in the right way. What do I mean by that?

Don't use LinkedIn as a tool to get introductions, but as a research database and then ask for an introduction via email, outside of LinkedIn.

Why? If you use the "Get introduced" function in LinkedIn you are the one who takes the initiative. The person you want to reach will get the message via someone he trusts (so that's a good thing), but you still took the initiative.

An action that generates way more trust is an email (or phone call) from someone they already know, like and trust who introduces you to each other!

Let's first look at two examples of such a Magic Email you can send yourself. In this way you understand the concept. Then we will look at how you can ask people from your network to send Magic Emails for you.

Example 1: introduce or refer a possible supplier and customer to each other

This is an (imaginary) example of an introduction or referral email (or the Magic Email):

To: eric.rogers@best-accounant-in-the-world.com

Cc: john.johnson@web-designer-number-one.com

Subject: introduction

HI Eric,

I want to introduce you to John Johnson (in cc). John is the Managing Director of Web Designer Number One. John may be the guy that can help you out with your new website. They make great websites (on their website www.web-designer-number-one.com you find lots of examples and references). I've known John for a while and even worked with him at ABC Company. One of the things I will always remember him by, is his ability to offer a solution that satisfies the needs of the customer while staying within the budget. He is really customer focused. I even recall him a few times recommending another solution or even another vendor if he thought it was in the interest of his customer. I definitely recommend him and his team!

John,

Eric Rogers is my accountant and also a personal friend. In fact, he is such a good accountant because he is more focused on people than on numbers! Eric is looking for a new website. And because of our joint experiences I thought you might be the perfect candidate."

I suggest the two of you get together for a talk. Maybe you can do this combined with watching a soccer game? I understood the both of you are fans of Manchester United.

Eric, you can reach John at: (telephone number John)

John, you can reach Eric at: (telephone number Eric)

Good luck!

Jan

Let's take a look at the "ingredients" of the Magic Email:

Header

- To: the person who is the "receiver" of the product, services or help.
- Cc: the person who is the "supplier" of the product, services or help.
- Subject: "introduction": this makes very clear what this email is about.

You can put more people in the "to" and "cc" field if that's appropriate. You can also put everybody in the "to" field, but for me this makes it easier to know who I introduced to whom. This is especially useful for your own "follow-up" or "stay in touch" actions.

Body

- **First I address the receiver then I address the supplier.**
- I always give the **reason** for connecting the both of them.
- After addressing the receiver I also always address the supplier so he knows **something about the receiver and especially about my relationship towards the receiver.** This makes it easier for him to find common ground. And to start the relationship on a much higher level than with a "cold call". In this example I even go a bit further: I go to the "value" level. Both are very customer and people focused. This is a very strong basis to build a relationship on. And especially when a third party with whom they both have a good relationship with points this out (which is me in this case).
- The same applies, of course, for the receiver with regard to the supplier.
- I include what I **appreciate** about the person, organization, product or service. This way I maintain and strengthen my relationship with every party. Even when there is no future interaction between them, the email was worth the effort as a "relationship building action".

- I also try to find **commonalities on another level than the professional one**. In this case they share a passion for soccer and they even support the same team. There is an instant bond. This bond exists most of the time (remember the 6 degrees of proximity), but we don't always find it in a conversation because we didn't talk about the areas where we might be related. If you as the connector know about the interests that two people share, tell them. This way you help them to get a flying start.
- **Include other references and objective parties if possible**. The better the receiver knows them the better the reputation of the supplier. In this example I referred to the references at the website of Web Designer Number One.

Conclusion:

- **Call to action: I suggest that they contact each other**. This means:
  - THEY are expected to take ACTION, and there are no barriers to do this, because I (the respected and trusted third party) suggested them to do this.
  - I put the telephone number of the "supplier" first, because I want to encourage the "receiver" to make contact. This is more comfortable for the "supplier". This way I try to decrease the feeling of "selling" something as much as possible. And I open the possibilities of building a relationship and helping each other out.
  - They contact EACH OTHER, not me anymore. I step out of the process. I did my part of the job: connecting them. Now it's up to them. This helps me to spend my time wisely as I'm not the intermediary.
- **Telephone contact data**: so they can quickly reach each other. If they want to have contact via email, they already have it in the header of the email. I don't recommend following up on an introduction like this via email. The way is wide open for a personal contact via the telephone.

For some people this example might be perceived as too pushy. Please note that this is an email to two people you already know and have a good relationship with. In this case I am very confident that bringing them together will be beneficial for both of them.

Example 2: Send a general introduction or referral email

If you are not a small business owner, freelancer or sales representative, you may ask yourself: how does the previous example apply to my situation?

Frankly, it is the same. You can always connect people as in the previous example. Helping your network is not only useful for the future, but it is also fun and very satisfying.

Let me give you an example of people working in the same, large organization. If you work in a small organization, you're better off doing the introductions in person and face-to-face.

The example of making an introduction within a large organization goes like this:

To: Thomas.Hunter@company-abc.com

Cc: Sue.Allen@company-abc.com

Subject: introduction

HI Thomas,

I want to introduce you to Sue Allen (in cc). Sue is one of the team members of the Eureca project. As you know the Eureca project faced lots of challenges with legislation changing and some team members being moved to other countries. But you know the saying "a challenge is a way to grow". And that's exactly what happened to Sue. Sue got the daunting task to take over part of the project regarding legislation. And she did that really well! I experienced her knowledge myself when I had to deal with the local law in a number of Asian countries. Sue does know very much about this and has built a good network to support her. I definitely recommend her for your next project!

Sue,

Thomas Hunter is one of our international project leaders. I know he has had difficulties in the past finding the right people for his team with regard to local legislation. He is now assembling the team for his next project and I think your expertise will benefit this project. Thomas is a great man to work with. I enjoyed the way he leads his teams: he supports his team members in every way he can and encourages them to take responsibility. He is also very good at delegating decision power to his team members. As you know I find this very important myself. In my opinion he is one of the best project leaders of our company.

In addition of a possible professional match, you will have lots to talk about your shared passion for winter holidays and more specifically snowboarding.

I suggest the two of you get together for a talk.

Thomas, you can reach Sue at: (telephone number Sue)

Sue, you can reach Thomas at: (telephone number Thomas)

Good luck!

Jan

You see that it is not that difficult to introduce or refer people via email. Make a habit of doing this yourself!

How to ask for a Magic Email?

Now you have seen the value of such an email, you might ask: "How do I ask for a Magic Email? How can I have other people sending such emails for me?"

In the Everlasting Referrals Home Study Course© I describe the 9 step Everlasting Referrals Question Sequence©. However, you don't need to go through this whole sequence to get a positive response. What the sequence does is generate not one, but several possible connections and emails.

Let me give you an example of how you can easily ask for an introduction to one person via a Magic Email.

In October 2005 I was one of the guest speakers at the Young European Entrepreneurs Regatta. One of the participating teams was from Mobistar (the second largest mobile telephone operator in Belgium and part of the Orange group). One of the team members was Vincent De Waele. He and I had a conversation there and he was interested in the principles behind networking. So I gave him some tips at that moment, but after the Regatta we didn't really stay in touch.

Several months later I met Vincent again at an Ecademy event (this is another online business network that you might be interested in joining since they also organize face-to-face meetings, see www.ecademy.com). It was the last Tuesday of June 2006. After a warm hello and a small update about what was going on in our lives Vincent told me that he was one of my biggest fans. "How do you mean?" was my question. "Well I have already

bought many copies of your book to give to people from my department."
Vincent said. "Well that is very nice." I responded. Vincent continued: "The
reason why I bought the books is that it is important for people who work
in a large and ever changing environment like Mobistar to have a good
network for their own career and to deliver their projects on time and within
budget." And he went on to tell me more reasons. After he stopped talking
about the reasons, I asked him: "**Vincent, if networking is so important
for the Mobistar employees, could you do Mobistar and me a favor and
connect me with the training manager by introducing us to each other
via one email?"**

"Yes, of course, it will be my pleasure," Vincent replied. And indeed, two days
later his email arrived. One day later on Friday morning I got a phone call
from Ann Rutten, training manager at Mobistar asking if we could see each
other to talk about networking training courses for their company. The next
Monday we had that meeting and a day later we planned the dates for a trial
session. Since that day we have been giving networking training courses for
Mobistar on a regular basis (and I hope we will be able to continue delivering
them for a long time for this valued customer).

Why do I give this example? To show you how easy it is to ask someone to
write such an email. It doesn't take much time or cost any money, so why
wouldn't people write such emails?

I can already hear you say: "But Jan, nobody has ever written an email like
that for me." That might be true, but have you ever asked someone to do
this? And moreover do you share your goals with people?

We all want to help other people and especially if it doesn't cost us any
money and only a small amount of time (like writing an email). But we have
to know how we can help each other. We have to know the goals of other
people.

So look back at your goal and ask the people who can connect you with
the persons in the first column to write a Magic Email for you. You will be
surprised by the help you will get!

> **Extra tip**: we talked in the Fundamental Principle of the Networking
> Attitude and the first angle of the Golden Triangle about giving and
> sharing. The easiest thing you can share with others are your contacts.
> So start writing Magic Emails for other people and you will soon
> experience how you will receive things back from your network.

The Magic Email via LinkedIn

You don't actually have to write an email, but can use LinkedIn to connect two people with each other (assuming of course they are both on LinkedIn).

How do you do that?

- In the left menu go to "Inbox/Compose Message"

- Put the people you want to connect in the "To" box. You can choose to start typing their first or last name (a list will pop up) or use your list of connections to choose from (click the "In" icon).

Still I suggest to write a "regular" email or ask someone to introduce you to the person you are looking for using a "regular" email. Why?

- Not everybody who is on LinkedIn already uses it on a frequent basis.

- A regular email still has another feeling and works better than an introduction via LinkedIn. But, of course, it is more important to make or receive the connection than the medium you use.

The Power of LinkedIn

Have you done the goal setting exercise? If you are like me you skipped the exercise and want to read on. Who am I to stop you? But it will make a huge difference to experience what the power of LinkedIn is when you have done the exercise. So do the exercise if you haven't done it yet, otherwise read on.

Now let's dive into the real power of LinkedIn. What is that power? LinkedIn makes connections visible between people. Many people say: "So what? I know I can browse through the connections of the people from my first degree network (if they haven't blocked this function, but only few people do). But how does that help me?"

When you start from a goal, you can approach it from a different way. You don't start from your network to look who they know, but you start from the people who are in the best position to help you reach your goals and then see via whom you are connected to them.

Since LinkedIn only shows the names of people when they are linked to you via your connections, it is important to have a good foundation. If you followed the steps in the previous chapter you have this foundation.

So what is our next step?

We are going to use the Search function of LinkedIn.

As already mentioned, there are a few different search functions. For the sake of this exercise we only focus on the Advanced Search function.

Where to find it? Click on "People" on the top left hand side menu or use the Search box at the top (click on Advanced next to it).

Now let's look at a few situations you can encounter and what to do on LinkedIn.

Situation 1: you know the name of the person.

If you know the name of the person who is in the best position to help you reach your goal, fill in his first and last name.

Now you can have two results: you either find the person or not.

- If you don't find the person this means that he doesn't have a Profile on LinkedIn. It used to be that you couldn't find someone when he was not in your first three degrees, but now you get the message "out of your network". This is an improvement. The disadvantage is that you still can't get introduced to this person, but you might find some information in his Profile that can help you guess which LinkedIn Groups he might be a member of. It is still a lot of guesswork and there may be some extra actions you need to take, but if you really want to connect with this person it might be worth your while.

- If you do find the person you will see how many degrees he is away from you and how many connections he has. If he has only a few connections, he is probably not using LinkedIn. In that case, don't have too much expectation of interactions on LinkedIn with this person. But you do have an alternative: the Magic Email. Ask your mutual contact to introduce you to each other using regular email.

Let's assume you have found the person. What is your next action?

- Click on the name. His Profile is shown.

- Scroll down a little bit. On the right hand side you see a box "How you're connected to *name*". Here you can see the connections between the two of you. This is where the power of LinkedIn resides: visualizing the connections.

- The next step is getting in touch with this person. There are two ways to do this: via LinkedIn or outside LinkedIn.

    o   If you want to go via LinkedIn, click on "Get introduced through a connection" on the top right hand side.

    o   If you have more than one mutual contact, choose the connection you want to forward your message and click "Continue". If you only have one mutual contact LinkedIn does this step automatically for you.

    o   Now you have to choose a message title and category and write two messages. One message for the end recipient and one for your first degree contact. Be aware that everybody who is in the chain can read both messages! So be always professional in your messages to your first degree network even if they are your best friend and you enjoy partying with them.

    o   What happens next? Your message is sent to your first degree contact. He can then decide whether or not to forward your message. You can always see at which point of the chain (= which person) your message is.

Big remark: if you found out that the person you are looking for, is a second degree contact, DO NOT use the "Get introduced through a connection" function of LinkedIn. Why? Because the action comes from you. You still have to take the initiative.

What is the alternative? Go outside of LinkedIn. Use LinkedIn as a research database and then take your communication outside LinkedIn. What are the steps to take?

- Look who is your first degree contact that you know the best.
- Call this first degree contact on the telephone.
- Explain your situation and ask this person to write a Magic Email where he introduces you and the person you are looking for to each other.

Why is this so powerful? Because the Magic Email doesn't come from you, but from a trusted third party. The recipient will be much more open to this than to a message from you, even if it is forwarded by someone he knows.

However, if the person you are looking for is a third degree contact, you only can go via LinkedIn because you don't see who is in between your first degree and the recipient.

Note: "if it is really important you can ask your first degree to look this person up on LinkedIn. Maybe you know the 'invisible' person, but are not directly linked."

Situation 2: you don't know the name of the person, but you know which function you are looking for or have other information to find him.

If you don't know the name of the person who is in the best position to help you reach your goal, but you do know his function or other information to find him, use other parameters in your search.

In the "People Search" screen you have several options to refine your search. These are the options:

- **Keywords:** here you can fill in everything you want. LinkedIn then searches on all fields (free text and lists).

- **Location:** anywhere (default) or located near. Remark: LinkedIn works with geographic areas and not with specific towns.

- **First Name and Last Name**: self-explanatory.

- **Title**: function. Interesting option is that you can choose to only receive people who are currently holding that position, people who had that position in the past or both (default).

- **Company**: interesting option is that you can choose to only receive people who are currently working for this company, people who worked for that company in the past or both (default).

- **School**: self-explanatory.

- **Industry**: you can search in all industries or one or more specific ones.

- **Groups**: you can search in all the groups you are a member of or one or more specific ones.

- **Interested In**: any user (default) or the specific kind of Profile this person listed he is interested in to connect with.

- **Joined your network**: anytime (default) or a shorter time period.

- **Sort by**: how the search results are sorted:

- ○ **Relevance** (default)

- ○ **Relationship + Recommendations (formerly "Degrees and recommendations")**: use this option if you are looking for a supplier or partner. The recommendations can give you a first impression.

- ○ **Relationship (formerly "degrees away from you")**: use this option if you are not looking for someone specific. Second degree contacts are easier to reach (via the Magic Email) than third degree contacts.

- ○ **Keywords**

- • **Views:** how the search results are presented: expanded (default) or basic. The difference between the two is that the expanded view gives extra current and past functions.

Now you can have two results: you either find the person or not. If you have found the person, see situation 1 for the steps to take.

If you haven't found this person, the reason might again be that he doesn't have a Profile on LinkedIn. However, there can be other reasons:

- • He filled in another function other than the one you are looking for. For example, maybe you typed in Human Resources Director while he filled in HR Manager. So use different descriptions of a function if you don't find him.

- • You used other parameters in your search other than he used in his Profile. Play with the options by refining your search on the right hand side (or change the sort options at the top of the search results). Maybe he doesn't hold the same position anymore (change the "current & past" option) or moved to another company (change the "current & past" option). Or maybe he listed himself under another category other than you are using to find him.

Conclusion of this chapter

In this chapter you did the GAIN exercise: you set a goal, listed the people in the best position to help you reach your goal and got some help from other people with extra input for your table.

You also learned what the most powerful tool is to use next to LinkedIn: the Magic Email.

We ended this chapter to use the information of the GAIN exercise to tap into the power of LinkedIn: we looked up the people from our table on LinkedIn whether by name or by function, found out who our mutual contacts were and asked them to make a connection for us using the Magic Email.

I truly hope you did the GAIN exercise and used it to experiment to experience what LinkedIn can do for you. If you did it you will be convinced of the power of LinkedIn. You will also understand the tips in the next chapter about advanced strategies much better.

LinkedIn Advanced Strategies

Before starting to read this chapter, be sure you have read the previous ones. The reason is that the Advanced Strategies build further on the strategy from the previous chapters.

The rest of this chapter is divided by the type of question people are having. These are the topics:

- Find a new customer *(p. 93)*

- Find a new employee *(p. 99)*

- Find a new job (or internship) *(p. 105)*

- Find a new supplier, partner or expert *(p. 112)*

- Find someone (internal) for help on a project *(p. 117)*

- Get more value from your referral or network club membership *(p. 123)*

- Increase the membership value and increase the amount of members of a (professional) organization as an organizer *(p. 128)*

So pick the topic that suits your situation the best and read that part. Of course you can always come back and read the advanced strategies for the other topics as well. Since most people only will read one piece of this chapter, you will notice when you read another piece that there is some repetition.

9 Advanced Strategies to Find a New Customer

Your network is your most powerful and cheapest aid to find new customers. Let's look at some advanced strategies on how to tap into the power of your network to find and get connected with them.

Strategy 1: Make a Definition of Your Customers/ Prospects

To find a new customer, the first step to take is setting goals like we did in the previous chapter. Normally when defining a sales goal you will also make a good definition of your prospects.

Take these things into account: what type of industry are they in? Which geographic location? Which functions or titles do the people you have contact with? Which other parameters do you have? Remember to use several synonyms of the function or title you are looking for. Also don't limit yourself to the decision makers, also write down the function of the influencers.

Maybe you already have a name of a person or a company from your prospect list. That is already good information you can use to find the right people.

Strategy 2: Find More Prospects

These are some additional strategies you can use to find more prospects:

1. **Browse in the networks of your current customers**. Chances are that they are connected with their colleagues in other departments in the same country, affiliations in other countries and with their counterparts in other companies.

2. **Look in their Profile at "Viewers of this Profile also viewed"**: in this way you might find other prospects. You can find this at the right hand side at the bottom of someone's Profile.

3. **Join the Groups where your customers and prospects are members.** Look in the Profile of your connections; the Groups are at the bottom. In Groups you can also find people who are not in your first three degrees. An extra advantage of being a member of the same Group is that you are able to contact them directly (many people turn the general option of being open for direct contacts on LinkedIn off, but not in the Groups they are a member of).

4. **Look in "Companies" in the top menu of every page**. This might give you additional information about your prospects. Not all companies are in this directory however, only the larger ones are for the moment, but this is a feature that is expanding.
    Look especially at "Divisions". If the company you are looking at is already a customer, their divisions might be additional customers. It always surprises me how many times the wheel is reinvented and how poor communication about suppliers is between departments and divisions. The bigger the organization, the more true this is. So use LinkedIn to find the people in these other divisions.

Strategy 3: Look your Customers and Prospects up on LinkedIn

Using the information from steps 1 and 2 you can do a search like we described in the previous chapter and ask the mutual connection to connect you with your prospect via a Magic Email.

But what do you do after the connection is made?

Remember that LinkedIn is a NETWORK platform and not a SALES platform.

This means that after you have received an introduction to a prospect you have to start building a relationship with them, not bombard them with sales calls and brochures.

So think about how you can help them. Think about what you can give or share with them without expecting anything in return without crossing your own boundaries. (For a list of things you can offer to other people I refer you to my book, "Let's Connect!")

Strategy 4: Join Groups

After making a good definition of your customers and prospects it becomes much easier to choose which associations to join in real life. And also which Groups to join on LinkedIn.

You can search for Groups in the Groups Directory.

If you still don't know which Groups to join or which Groups your prospects might be a member of, tap into the intelligence of LinkedIn: look in the Profile of your current customers which Groups they are a member of. You might be surprised!

Once you are a member of a Group, remember it is about building relationships and increasing your own visibility and credibility. You can do this by contributing in the Discussion forums. Again, remember the forums are a place to help people and to give them advice, not to sell your products or services. When giving advice and help, your Know, Like and Trust factor will increase.

Other interesting Groups to join are Groups of other sales people or business owners in your region. Not only can you learn from each other, but also if you build a relationship with them by again contributing in Discussions, they might send some business your way.

Strategy 5: Answer Questions

Another way of increasing your visibility and credibility is answering questions in the Answer section of LinkedIn. You can make yourself stand out by the quality of your answers in the first place.

If the people who are asking questions consider you as the one with the best answer, they can also award you expert points. Depending on the category you are answering questions in this can quickly lead to extra visibility when you are on the Expert list.

A small note: at the time of writing there were only topic related categories. This means there was no connection with a specific geographic location or industry. So it depends on where your target group is and how active it is related to Answers whether it is worth your while or not.

Strategy 6: Increase your Number of Recommendations

As we said in Fundamental Principle Number 5: people do business with and refer business to people they know, like and trust.

What is interesting about trust is that it can be passed on. Or at least part of it. When you are looking for a plumber and a good friend of yours recommends one, don't you trust this person more?

LinkedIn also helps with that part: people can write Recommendations for each other. However, we are all so busy that most of us don't think about doing this spontaneously.

So how can you get more Recommendations? These are two strategies I suggest:

1. **Ask your current customers and colleagues for a Recommendation**. You can use the tools that LinkedIn provides, but I would suggest adding at least some other form of communication. In a face-to-face meeting or via the telephone bring up the Recommendations function of LinkedIn and ask them if they want to write a small Recommendation for you. Do this especially when you contact customers. For colleagues you can work with an email. Then you can send a reminder via LinkedIn in which you refer to your prior communication. You can do this under "Profile", "Recommendations" and then "Request Recommendation". Again don't use the standard request, but make it personal and refer in the text to your meeting or call. This way of working is more time intensive then using the standard LinkedIn message, but the results will also be much better. K eep in mind that only using the standard LinkedIn message to request a Recommendation without any other communication might put off the people you want to write a Recommendation. The result will then be the opposite of what you want to achieve: you will harm your relationships with your current customers and colleagues more than appearing more interesting for potential customers.

2. **Write a Recommendation for someone else first**. The standard message of LinkedIn after you have recommended someone (which you can't change) is an invitation to write a Recommendation for the person who just recommended you. Many people will do this. If you follow this strategy, always be honest and do not overly praise people you met only once. Then your chances to get a Recommendation back decrease. And if someone asks you later about this person you have to admit you don't know this person very well. This might harm your credibility with the third party.

Remarks:

- If you are not completely happy with the Recommendation because it is not accurate or too vague, you can ask them to modify the Recommendation. If after a modification you are still not happy, you can always choose not to show it on your Profile.

- Sometimes your contacts will reply that they don't know what to write. Then suggest you make a draft version that they can use to start from. If you are honest and don't exaggerate they will probably just post your draft version without changing anything.

Strategy 7: Use the "Status Update" function

The "Status Update" function allows you to share what you are doing right now. You have 100 characters.

How could this help you? If you are looking for a certain person or function you don't find on LinkedIn, you can mention this. This message is then shown to some or all people from your network. They might think of someone they know who is not on LinkedIn or who's Profile didn't match your search criteria.

You can choose who can see this "Status update": only your direct connections, your first three degrees or everyone. Depending on what you have written and who is in your network, you might change this every time you update your status.

Don't have too many expectations from this, not everybody reads these status updates and reacts on them. On the other hand, it only takes you a few seconds of your time and you never know who might help you.

Where to find this? Click in the left menu on "Profile", then in the white box under your picture you can update your status.

Remark: if you have also an account on other websites like Plaxo,

Facebook, MySpace or Twitter, there are now tools, which have you, update your status on all websites at the same time. See chapter "Free Tools to save you time when working with LinkedIn".

Strategy 8: Watch the Network Updates

The Network Updates on your LinkedIn Home Page might give you interesting information.

For example, when someone changes position at your customer or at a prospect. Then you can take action to see if you can be a supplier to the new company of your contact and also to be introduced to the person he is replaced by. When someone at a prospect who didn't buy from you changes position or leaves the company this might be an opportunity to get a new chance.

It is also interesting to see who joins the Groups you are a member of. This person might be new to LinkedIn and not connected to your network. So you won't be able to connect with them via your LinkedIn network. But you can connect with him via the Group.

See who is asking questions. And also who is answering them. This might give you information about specific situations at certain organizations or general tendencies in the marketplace.

It might also be interesting to see who is connecting to whom. If you suddenly see that a prospect and a good business contact are connected, you might ask your contact to introduce you (or even recommend you) to this prospect.

Finally, it also can keep you awake. When you see that one of your conculleagues connected to one of your current customers, it might be a good alert to call them again or pay them a visit.

Strategy 9: Use LinkedIn as a potential lead generator by creating alerts

LinkedIn offers the possibility to save your searches and run them automatically for you. In the free account there are 3 saved search slots. You can run them manually or have them run automatically every week or month.

Why can this be useful for you? After you have made a definition of your customer(s) and have experimented with the search function to find them, you can save this search and have it automatically run by LinkedIn. Every week or month LinkedIn will email you the new people who match the criteria in your saved search.

By now you understand the power of LinkedIn and how it can take your sales to the next level(s). If you want even more tips on how to create a network of "ambassadors" that bring in customer after customer so you won't ever have to cold call again, take a look at our Everlasting Referrals Home Study Course: www.everlasting-referrals.com

11 Advanced Strategies to Find a New Employee or Candidate

Your network is your most powerful and cheapest aid to find new employees and candidates. Let's look at some advanced strategies on how to tap into the power of your network to find a new employee or candidate.

Strategy 1: Make a Definition of the new Employee/Candidate

To find a new employee or candidate, the first step to take is setting goals like we did in the previous chapter. Normally when defining that goal you will make a good definition of the employees or candidates you are looking for.

Take these things into account: what type of industry are they in? Which geographic location? Which functions or titles do they need to have? Think about current and past functions. Which other parameters do you have? Remember to use several synonyms of the function or expertise you are looking for!

Maybe you already have names of specific people on a list. That is already good information you can use to find the right people.

Strategy 2: Find More Candidates

These are some additional strategies you can use to find more candidates:

1. **Browse in the networks of your current contacts with a similar function or role**. Chances are that they are connected with their colleagues in other departments in the same country, affiliations in other countries and with their counterparts in other organizations. Also read in their Profiles about the words they use to describe their expertise. You can learn some new words or find synonyms in your search.

2. **Look in the Profile of your candidates at "Viewers of this Profile also viewed"**: in this way you might find other candidates. You can find this at the right hand side at the bottom of someone's Profile.

3. **Join the Groups where your candidates are a member of.** Look in the Profile of your connections; the Groups are at the bottom. In Groups you can also find people who are not in your first three degrees. An extra advantage of being a member of the same Group is that you are able to contact them directly (many people turn the general option of being open for direct contacts on LinkedIn off, but not in the Groups they are a member of).

4. **Look in "Companies" in the top menu of every page**. This might give you additional information about the companies people have worked for or are working for. Not all companies are in this directory, however, only the larger ones.

Strategy 3: Look your Candidates up on LinkedIn

Using the information from steps 1 and 2 you can do a search like we described in the previous chapter and ask the mutual connection to connect you with your candidate via a Magic Email.

But what do you do after the connection is made?

Remember that the power of networking is in the second degree. So don't only focus on the person you have found, but also ask for introductions to other people he or she might know.

Strategy 4: Use the LinkedIn Jobs tools

LinkedIn offers several tools to help you find a candidate.

To get started, click on "Jobs" in the top menu. Then click on "Need to Fill a Position" on the top right hand side. Or alternatively click on the arrow next to "Jobs" in the top menu and select "Hiring Home".

On this page you will see three options:

- **Post a job today**: this takes you to the page where you can post a job. There are some interesting parameters that can be used:

  - **In additional information** you can choose one or more of these options:

    - Applicants with Recommendations preferred

    - Referrals through my network preferred

- Local candidates only, no relocation

- Third party applications not accepted

  o When you post a job, you can choose to include your Profile or not. A next step after posting a job can be distributing it via your network on LinkedIn. Including your Profile can give you extra visibility in your network. LinkedIn also says "*Listings with Profiles receive special promotion to candidates in your network.*"

- **Upgrade to find more candidates**: when you upgrade you are not limited to your first three degrees anymore and you are also able to contact people directly.

- **Empower your corporate staffing**: LinkedIn has extra tools for recruitment teams.

Strategy 5: Reference Search

After you have found a candidate LinkedIn also allows you to do a reference search (when you have a Business or Pro account).

Click on "People" and then on the tab "Reference Search".

Next you can fill in the name of a company and a time period (between year x and year y). LinkedIn will then return everybody who worked for that company during those years.

You can then contact some of the people you have found to find out more about a candidate.

Strategy 6: Join Groups

After making the definition of what a good candidate looks like it becomes much easier to choose which associations to join in real life. And also which Groups to join on LinkedIn.

You can search for Groups in the Groups Directory.

If you still don't know which Groups to join or which Groups your candidates might be a member of, tap into the intelligence of LinkedIn: look in the Profile of your current candidates and people who you have recruited which Groups they are a member of. You might be surprised!

Once you are a member of a Group, remember it is about building relationships and increasing your own visibility and credibility. You can do this by contributing in the Discussion forums. Again, remember the forums are a place to help people and to give them advice, not to recruit people. When giving advice and help, your know, like and trust factor will increase.

Other interesting Groups to join are Groups of other recruiters in your region. Not only can you learn from each other, but also if you build a relationship with them by again contributing in Discussions, they might send some candidates your way.

Strategy 7: Answer Questions

Another way of increasing your visibility and credibility is answering questions in the Answer section of LinkedIn. You can make yourself stand out by the quality of your answers in the first place.

If the people who are asking questions consider you as the one with the best answer, they can also award you expert points. Depending on the category you are answering questions in this can quickly lead to extra visibility when you are on the Expert list.

A small note: at the time of writing there were only topic related categories. This means there was no connection with a specific geographic location or industry. So it depends on where your target group is and how active it is related to Answers whether it is worth your while or not.

Why could this be useful as a recruiter? Not only to be more in the picture of possible customers if you are working for a recruitment agency, but also to give more confidence to the candidates you are contacting.

Strategy 8: Increase your Number of Recommendations

As we said in Fundamental Principle Number 5: people do business with and refer business to people they know, like and trust.

What is interesting about trust is that it can be passed on. Or at least part of it. When you are looking for a plumber and a good friend of yours recommends one, don't you trust this person more?

LinkedIn also helps with that part: people can write Recommendations for each other. However, we are all so busy that most of us don't think about doing this spontaneously.

So how can you get more Recommendations? These are two strategies

I suggest:

1. **Ask your current colleagues and the people you already have recruited for a Recommendation**. You can use the tools that LinkedIn provides, but I would suggest adding at least some other form of communication. In a face-to-face meeting or via the telephone bring up the Recommendations function of LinkedIn and ask them if they want to write a small Recommendation for you. Do this especially when you contact people you have recruited in the past or customers you have worked for in the past. For colleagues you can work with an email.
Then you can send a reminder via LinkedIn in which you refer to your prior communication. You can do this under "Profile", "Recommendations" and then "Request Recommendation". Again, don't use the standard request, but make it personal and refer in the text to your meeting or call. This way of working is more time intensive then using the standard LinkedIn message, but the results will also be much better. Keep in mind that only using the standard LinkedIn message to request a Recommendation without any other communication might put off the people you want to write a Recommendation. The result will be then the opposite of you want to achieve: you will harm your relationships with your current contacts more than appearing more interesting for potential candidates.

2. **Write a Recommendation for someone else first**. The standard message of LinkedIn after you have recommended someone (which you can't change) is an invitation to write a Recommendation for the person who just recommended you. Many people will do this. If you follow this strategy, always be honest and do not overly praise people you met only once. Then your chances to get a Recommendation back decrease. And if someone asks you later about this person you have to admit you don't know this person very well. This might harm your credibility with the third party.

Remarks:

- If you are not completely happy with the Recommendation because it is not accurate or too vague, you can ask them to modify the Recommendation. If after a modification you are still not happy, you can always choose not to show it on your Profile.

- Sometimes your contacts will reply that they don't know what to write. Then suggest you make a draft version that they can use to start from. If you are honest and don't exaggerate they will probably just post your draft version without changing anything.

Strategy 9: Use the "Status Update" function

The "Status Update" function allows you to share what you are doing right now. You have 100 characters.

How could this help you? If you are looking for a certain person or function you don't find on LinkedIn, you can mention this. This message is then shown to some or all people from your network. They might think of someone they know who is not on LinkedIn or who's Profile didn't match your search criteria.

You can choose who can see this "Status update": only your direct connections, your first three degrees or everyone. Depending on what you have written and who is in your network, you might change this every time you update your status.

Don't have too many expectations from this, not everybody reads these status updates and reacts on them. On the other hand, it only takes you a few seconds of your time and you never know who might help you.

Where to find this? Click in the left menu on "Profile", then in the white box under your picture you can update your status.

Remark: if you have an account on other websites like Plaxo, Facebook, MySpace or Twitter, there are now tools, which have you, update your status on all websites at the same time. See chapter "Free Tools to save you time when working with LinkedIn".

Strategy 10: Watch the Network Updates

The Network Updates on your LinkedIn Home Page might give you interesting information.

For example, when someone took a course or moves to another country. Suddenly he might be a potential candidate.

It is also interesting to see who joins the Groups you are a member of. This person might be new to LinkedIn and not connected to your network. So you won't be able to connect with them via your LinkedIn network. But you can connect with him via the Group.

See who is asking questions. And also who is answering them. This might give you information about specific situations at an organization or general tendencies in the marketplace.

Finally it might also be interesting to see who is connecting to whom. If you suddenly see that a candidate and a contact are connected, you might ask your contact to introduce you to the candidate.

Strategy 11: Use LinkedIn as a potential candidate generator by creating alerts

LinkedIn offers the possibility to save your searches and run them automatically for you. In the free account there are 3 saved search slots. You can run them manually or have them run automatically every week or month.

Why can this be useful for you? After you have made a definition of your candidate(s) and have experimented with the search function to find them, you can save this search and have it automatically run by LinkedIn. Every week or month LinkedIn will email you the new people who match the criteria in your saved search.

12 Advanced Strategies to Find a New Job or Internship

Your network is one of the best aids to help you find a new job. The Advanced Strategies I describe here are focused on finding a first job or internship or a job in another company. However, the tips can also help you when you are looking for a new job in your current company. If you are looking for another job in the same organization, also read the Advanced Strategies to Find Internal or External Expertise.

Strategy 1: Make a Definition of the Job you want

To find a new job, the first step to take is setting goals like we did in the previous chapter. Normally when defining that goal you will make a good definition of the job you are looking for.

Take these things into account: what type of industry? Which geographic location? Which functions or titles are you interested in? Which kind of projects do you want to work on? What do you want to earn? Maybe you already have one or more names of specific organizations you want to work for? Which other parameters do you have? Remember to use several synonyms of the function you are looking for!

Strategy 2: Find More People who can help you find a new job

These are some additional strategies you can use to find more people who can help you find a new job:

1. **Browse in the networks of your current contacts with a similar function or role or who work for the organization you want to work for.** Chances are that they are connected with their colleagues

in other departments in the same country, affiliations in other countries and with their counterparts in other organizations. Also read in their Profiles about the words they use to describe their expertise. You can learn some new words or find synonyms in your search.

2. **Look in the Profile of someone who might help you find a new job at "Viewers of this Profile also viewed"**: in this way you might find other people who might help you. You can find this at the right hand side at the bottom of someone's Profile.

3. **Join the Groups where the people who have the function you want or who work in the industry you want to work in are a member of.** Look in the Profile of your connections; the Groups are at the bottom. In Groups you can also find people who are not in your first three degrees. An extra advantage of being a member of the same Group is that you are able to contact them directly (many people turn the general option of being open for direct contacts on LinkedIn off, but not in the Groups they are a member of).

4. **Look in "Companies" in the top menu of every page.** This might give you additional information about the companies you would like to work for and the people have worked for them or are still working for them. Not all companies are in this directory however, only the larger ones.

5. **Look also for the career coordinator of the college or university you went to (or are going to)**: Mary Roll, career coordinator for the international MBA program at Vlerick Leuven Gent Management School mentioned that career coordinators not only work for current students, but also for alumni. Career coordinators are a very valuable resource since they are continuously in touch with several companies and organizations.

Strategy 3: Look up the people who might help you on LinkedIn

Using the information from steps 1 and 2 you can do a search like we described in the previous chapter and ask the mutual connection to connect you with them via a Magic Email.

But what do you do after the connection is made?

Remember that the power of networking is in the second degree. So the best advice I can give you when you are looking for a new job is to ask for advice.

Ask the people you get in touch with for advice what they would do if they were in your situation.

This approach works like a charm! Why? Because people love to share advice. They also open more up to you because you don't want anything from them except advice.

What happens in practice many times is that they give you ideas you would never have thought of and they also often spontaneously suggest introducing you to other people.

If they do that, ask them to write a Magic Email for you.

Strategy 4: Use the LinkedIn Jobs tools

LinkedIn offers several tools to help you find a job.

To get started, click on "Jobs" in the top menu.

Then you can use a simple search (keywords and location) or an advanced search.

What the power of LinkedIn is, is that for every job that was posted on LinkedIn you can see which connections you have with that particular company. This tool is called the JobInsider.

What is the value of this knowledge?

- You can ask your first degree contacts at that company about some background information about the company.

- You can ask your first degree contacts at that company who are the people who are involved in the recruiting process.

- You can ask your first degree contacts at that company and other organizations to write you a Recommendation focused on the function you are interested in.

- You can ask your first degree contacts to introduce or recommend you to the people who are involved in the hiring process. Ask them to write a Magic Email for you. This works much better than getting a connection through LinkedIn.

When the job posting is only available on LinkedIn, you can apply for this job by using the form LinkedIn provides. You can write a cover letter (required) and upload your resume. Your LinkedIn Profile is automatically attached to the application. So make sure your Profile is up to date!

Strategy 5: Join Groups

After defining your ideal job it becomes much easier to choose which associations to join in real life. And also which Groups to join on LinkedIn.

You can search for Groups in the Groups Directory.

If you still don't know which Groups to join or which Groups the people who have the same function or are in the same industry you would like to work in are a member of, tap into the intelligence of LinkedIn: look in the Profile of your current contacts with a similar function or background which Groups they are a member of. You might be surprised!

Once you are a member of a Group, remember it is about building relationships and increasing your own visibility and credibility. You can do this by contributing in the Discussion forums. Again, remember the forums are a place to help people and to give them advice, not to apply for jobs. When giving advice and help, your Know, Like and Trust factor will increase.

Strategy 6: Answer Questions

Another way of increasing your visibility and credibility is answering questions in the Answer section of LinkedIn. You can make yourself stand out by the quality of your answers in the first place.

If the people who are asking questions consider you as the one with the best answer, they can also award you expert points. Depending on the category you are answering questions in this can quickly lead to extra visibility when you are on the Expert list.

A small note: at the time of writing there were only topic related categories. This means there was no connection with a specific geographic location or industry. So it depends on where your target group is and how active it is related to Answers whether it is worth your while or not.

Strategy 7: Increase your Number of Recommendations

As we said in Fundamental Principle Number 5: people do business with and refer business to people they know, like and trust.

What is interesting about trust is that it can be passed on. Or at least part of it. When you are looking for a plumber and a good friend of yours recommends one, don't you trust this person more?

LinkedIn also helps with that part: people can write Recommendations for each other. However, we are all so busy that most of us don't think about doing this spontaneously.

So how can you get more Recommendations? These are two strategies I suggest:

1. **Ask your former and current colleagues, classmates and former employers for a Recommendation**. You can use the tools that LinkedIn provides, but I would suggest adding at least some other form of communication. In a face-to-face meeting or via the telephone bring up the Recommendations function of LinkedIn and ask them if they want to write a small Recommendation for you. Do this especially when you contact people you have worked with in the past: former colleagues, bosses and summer job supervisors (if you are a student). For colleagues you can work with an email.
   Then you can send a reminder via LinkedIn in which you refer to your prior communication. You can do this under "Profile", "Recommendations" and then "Request Recommendation". Again don't use the standard request, but make it personal and refer in the text to your meeting or call. This way of working is more time intensive then using the standard LinkedIn message, but the results will also be much better. Keep in mind that only using the standard LinkedIn message to request a Recommendation without any other communication might put off the people you want to write a Recommendation. The result will then be the opposite of what you want to achieve: you will harm your relationships with your current contacts more than appearing more interesting for potential employers.

2. **Write a Recommendation for someone else first**. The standard message of LinkedIn after you have recommended someone (which you can't change) is an invitation to write a Recommendation for the person who just recommended you. Many people will do this. If you follow this strategy, always be honest and do not overly praise people you met only once. Then your chances to get a Recommendation back decrease. And If someone asks you later about this person you have to admit you don't know this person very well. This might harm your credibility with the third party.

Remarks:

- If you are not completely happy with the Recommendation because it is not accurate or too vague, you can ask them to modify the Recommendation. If after a modification you are still not happy, you can always choose not to show it on your Profile.

- Sometimes your contacts will reply that they don't know what to write. Then suggest you make a draft version that they can use to start from. If you are honest and don't exaggerate they will probably just post your draft version without changing anything.

Strategy 8: Use the "Status Update" function

The "Status Update" function allows you to share what you are doing right now. You have 100 characters.

How could this help you? Share the job you are looking for or if you are looking for a certain person or function who could help you, but whom you don't find on LinkedIn, you can mention this. This message is then shown to some or all people from your network. They might think of someone they know who is not on LinkedIn or who's Profile didn't match your search criteria.

You can choose who can see this "Status update": only your direct connections, your first three degrees or everyone. Depending on what you have written and who is in your network, you might change this every time you update your status.

Don't have too many expectations from this, not everybody reads these status updates and reacts on them. On the other hand, it only takes you a few seconds of your time and you never know who might help you.

Where to find this? Click in the left menu on "Profile", then in the white box under your picture you can update your status.

Remark: if you have also an account on other websites like Plaxo, Facebook, MySpace or Twitter, there are now tools, which have you, update your status on all websites at the same time. See chapter "Free Tools to save you time when working with LinkedIn".

Strategy 9: Use the JobInsider function of the LinkedIn Browser Toolbar

Download the free Internet Explorer or Firefox Toolbar, which can be found at the bottom of every page under "Tools" (Note: clicking on the "JobInsider" tool leads to the same Browser Toolbar).

After installing the Toolbar these are the tools that are available in the browser:

- **Search bar**: search in LinkedIn from the toolbar (so you don't have to go to the website).

- **Bookmarks**: after you have bookmarked some Profiles on LinkedIn, you can manage them from here.

- **JobInsider**: opens up a new pane in your browser. When looking at job postings in your normal browser window you can use this extra pane to look up how you are connected to people from the organization you are interested in. This is the same tool as we discussed in strategy 4 (the same content), but it is used in a different way. In strategy 4 it is embedded in the LinkedIn search, while here it is an extra pane in your browser that is separate from your actions on LinkedIn and which can be used while browsing websites other than LinkedIn.

As you see the JobInsider tool makes it easier to find the people that can help you get a job.

Strategy 10: Watch the Network Updates

The Network Updates on your LinkedIn Home Page might give you interesting information.

For example, when there is a new recruiter at the company you want to work for or if someone who recruited you in the past changes companies.

It is also interesting to see who joins the Groups you are a member of. This person might be new to LinkedIn and not connected to your network. So you won't be able to connect with them via your LinkedIn network. But you can connect with him via the Group.

See who is asking questions. And also who is answering them. This might give you information about specific situations at the companies you want to work for or general tendencies in the marketplace.

Finally, it might also be interesting to see who is connecting to whom. If you suddenly see that a recruiter or someone else at the company you want to work for connects with a good business contact, you might ask your contact to introduce you (or even recommend you) to your prospect.

Strategy 11: Connect with other Job Seekers

If you are in a program with other people who are looking for a new job, it is also a good idea to connect with each other on LinkedIn. In this way your network expands and you might find new opportunities.

If you are a student you might think you have a limited network. But when you start linking with these people, you already have a good basis to start from: fellow students, parents, family members, neighbors, people from the sport or hobby club, professors, guest lecturers, representatives of companies at Job Days, company visits or conferences, internship contacts, coordinator of the career program and people you know from other social networking websites like Facebook or MySpace.

Also make sure you make clear to each other when you see each other or via email what job you are looking for. They can be your ambassadors and you can be theirs.

Strategy 12: Create Alerts

LinkedIn offers the possibility to save your searches and run them automatically for you. In the free account there are 3 saved search slots. You can run them manually or have them run automatically every week or month.

Why can this be useful for you? After you have made a definition of a recruiter or HR responsible and have experimented with the search function to find them, you can save this search and have it automatically run by LinkedIn. Every week or month LinkedIn will email you the new people who match the criteria in your saved search.

10 Advanced Strategies to Find a New Supplier or Partnership

Your network is your most powerful and cheapest aid to find new suppliers or partners. Let's look at some advanced strategies on how to tap into the power of your network to find and get connected with them.

Strategy 1: Make a Definition of the new Supplier/Partner

To find a new supplier or partner, the first step to take is setting goals like we did in the previous chapter. Normally when defining that goal you will also make a good definition of the supplier or partner you are looking for.

Take these things into account: what type of industry are they in? Which geographic location? Which functions or titles do they need to have? Think about current and past functions. Which other parameters do you have? Remember to use several synonyms of the function or expertise you are looking for!

Maybe you already have a name of a person or a specific company on a list. That is already good information you can use to find the right people.

Strategy 2: Find More Potential Suppliers/Partners

These are some additional strategies you can use to find more potential suppliers or partners:

1. **Browse in the networks of your current contacts with a similar function or role**. Chances are that they are connected with their colleagues in other departments in the same country, affiliations in other countries and with their counterparts in other organizations. Also read in their Profiles about the words they use to describe their expertise. You can learn some new words or find synonyms in your search.

2. **Look in the Profile of potential suppliers or partners at "Viewers of this Profile also viewed"**: in this way you might find other potential suppliers or partners. You can find this at the right hand side at the bottom of someone's Profile.

3. **Join the Groups where your current suppliers or partners are a member of.** Look in the Profile of your connections; the Groups are at the bottom. In Groups you can also find people who are not in your first three degrees. An extra advantage of being a member of the same Group is that you are able to contact them directly (many people turn the general option of being open for direct contacts on LinkedIn off, but not in the Groups they are a member of).

4. **Look in "Companies" in the top menu of every page**. This might give you additional information about the companies people have worked for or are working for. Not all companies are in this directory, however, only the larger ones.

Strategy 3: Look your Potential Suppliers/Partners up on LinkedIn

Using the information from steps 1 and 2 you can do a search like we described in the previous chapter and ask the mutual connection to connect you with your potential supplier or partner via a Magic Email.

But what do you do after the connection is made?

Remember that the power of networking is in the second degree. So don't only focus on the person you have found, but also ask for introductions to other people.

Strategy 4: Join Groups

After defining your potential suppliers or partners it becomes much easier to choose which associations to join in real life. And also which Groups to join on LinkedIn.

You can search for Groups in the Groups Directory.

If you still don't know which Groups to join or which Groups your suppliers or partners might be a member of, tap into the intelligence of LinkedIn: look in the Profile of your current suppliers/partners which Groups they are a member of. You might be surprised!

Once you are a member of a Group, remember it is about building relationships and increasing your own visibility and credibility. You can do this by contributing in the Discussion forums. Again, remember the forums are a place to help people and to give them advice. When giving advice and help, your know, like and trust factor will increase.

Other interesting Groups to join are Groups of other purchasers or people with the same function in your region. Not only can you learn from each other, but also if you build a relationship with them by again contributing in Discussions, they might get you in touch with good suppliers or partners.

Strategy 5: Answer Questions

Another way of increasing your visibility and credibility is answering questions in the Answer section of LinkedIn. You can make yourself stand out by the quality of your answers in the first place.

If the people who are asking questions consider you as the one with the best answer, they can also award you expert points. Depending on the category you are answering questions in this can quickly lead to extra visibility when you are on the Expert list.

A small note: at the time of writing there were only topic related categories. This means there was no connection with a specific geographic location or industry. So it depends on where your target group is and how active it is related to Answers whether it is worth your while or not.

Strategy 6: Increase your Number of Recommendations

As we said in Fundamental Principle Number 5: people do business with and refer business to people they know, like and trust.

What is interesting about trust is that it can be passed on. Or at least part of it. When you are looking for a plumber and a good friend of yours recommends one, don't you trust this person more?

LinkedIn also helps with that part: people can write Recommendations for each other. However, we are all so busy that most of us don't think about doing this spontaneously.

So how can you get more Recommendations? These are two strategies I suggest:

1. **Ask your current colleagues and the people you already worked with in the past for a Recommendation**. You can use the tools that LinkedIn provides, but I would suggest adding at least some other form of communication. In a face-to-face meeting or via the telephone bring up the Recommendations function of LinkedIn and ask them if they want to write a small Recommendation for you. Do this especially when you contact people you have worked with in the past. For colleagues you can work with an email.
    Then you can send a reminder via LinkedIn in which you refer to your prior communication. You can do this under "Profile", "Recommendations" and then "Request Recommendation". Again, don't use the standard request, but make it personal and refer in the text to your meeting or call. This way of working is more time intensive then using the standard LinkedIn message, but the results will also be much better. Keep in mind that only using the standard LinkedIn message to request a Recommendation without any other communication might put off the people you want to write a Recommendation. The result will then be the opposite of what you want to achieve: you will harm your relationships with your current contacts more than appearing more interesting for potential suppliers and partners.

2. **Write a Recommendation for someone else first**. The standard message of LinkedIn after you have recommended someone (which you can't change) is an invitation to write a Recommendation for the person who just recommended you. Many people will do this. If you follow this strategy, always be honest and do not overly praise people you met only once. Then your chances to get a Recommendation back decrease. And if someone asks you later about this person you have to admit you don't know this person very well. This might harm your credibility with the third party.

Remarks:

*   If you are not completely happy with the Recommendation because it is not accurate or too vague, you can ask them to modify the Recommendation. If after a modification you are still not happy, you can always choose not to show it on your Profile.

*   Sometimes your contacts will reply that they don't know what to write. Then suggest you make a draft version that they can use to start from. If you are honest and don't exaggerate they will probably just post your draft version without changing anything.

Strategy 7: Use the "Status Update" function

The "Status Update" function allows you to share what you are doing right now. You have 100 characters.

How could this help you? If you are looking for a certain person or function you don't find on LinkedIn, you can mention this. This message is then shown to some or all people from your network. They might think of someone they know who is not on LinkedIn or who's Profile didn't match your search criteria.

You can choose who can see this "Status update": only your direct connections, your first three degrees or everyone. Depending on what you have written and who is in your network, you might change this every time you update your status.

Don't have too many expectations from this, not everybody reads these status updates and reacts on them. On the other hand, it only takes you a few seconds of your time and you never know who might help you.

Where to find this? Click in the left menu on "Profile" and then in the white box under your picture you can update your status.

Remark: if you also have an account on other websites like Plaxo, Facebook, MySpace or Twitter, there are now tools, which have you, update your status on all websites at the same time. See chapter "Free Tools to save you time when working with LinkedIn".

Strategy 8: Watch the Network Updates

The Network Updates on your LinkedIn Home Page might give you interesting information.

For example, when someone changes position at your current supplier or partner or changes companies. Then you can take action to see if you can work with the new company of your contact and also be introduced to the person he is replaced by.

It is also interesting to see who joins the Groups you are a member of. This person might be new to LinkedIn and not connected to your network. So you won't be able to connect with them via your LinkedIn network. But you can connect with him via the Group.

See who is asking questions. And also who is answering them. This might give you information about specific situations at your suppliers/partners or general tendencies in the marketplace.

Finally, it might also be interesting to see who is connecting to whom. If you suddenly see that a colleague or a current supplier/partner and a potential one are connected, you might ask the colleague or current supplier/partner to introduce you (or even recommend you) to your potential supplier/partner.

Strategy 9: Reference Search

After you have found someone at a supplier or partner LinkedIn also allows you to do a reference search (when you have a Business or Pro account).

Click on "People" and then on the tab "Reference Search".

Next you can fill in the name of a company and a time period (between year x and year y). LinkedIn will then return everybody who worked for that company during those years.

You can then contact some of the people you have found to find out more about a specific person at a potential supplier or partner.

Although most people wouldn't use or need this function, for some it might be an interesting one.

Strategy 10: Use LinkedIn as a potential supplier/partner generator by creating alerts

LinkedIn offers the possibility to save your searches and run them automatically for you. In the free account there are 3 saved search slots. You can run them manually or have them run automatically every week or month.

Why can this be useful for you? After you have made a definition of your supplier/partner and have experimented with the search function to find them, you can save this search and have it automatically run by LinkedIn. Every week or month LinkedIn will email you the new people who match the criteria in your saved search.

9 Advanced Strategies to Find Internal or External Expertise

Everybody is working on projects nowadays. Some are pretty straightforward, but for many projects we need the advice or expertise of others. Or from another point of view: if we had access to this advice or expertise it would give us better results in less time. Sometimes we need more than advice: people working on a project. The question is many times: where and how do I find the right expertise and the right people? We know that they are somewhere, and maybe even in our network, but how can we find them?

From an organizational point of view, tapping into the knowledge of a network is a very good remedy against large costs from reinventing the wheel.

LinkedIn can provide a large part of the solution to find both internal and external expertise. The reasons?

- LinkedIn has more elaborate Profiles than most internal directories (which are sometimes also limited to one country). So it is easier to find someone and to see at a glance if this is the person you need.

- LinkedIn shows the Profiles from people in other large organizations and from freelance experts. Without LinkedIn they would be harder to find.

- LinkedIn shows the connections between people and also the Recommendations people received. This will also allow helping you to make a quick decision on whom to contact.

Now that we know the value of LinkedIn to find internal and external expertise, let's look at some advanced strategies to find the experts.

Strategy 1: Make a Definition of the Expert

To find an internal or external expert, the first step to take is setting goals like we did in the previous chapter. Normally when defining that goal you will also make a good definition of the expert you need.

Take these things into account: what type of industry are they in? Which geographic location? Which functions or titles do they have? Which projects have they worked on the past? Which departments? Which other parameters do you have? Remember to use several synonyms of the function or expertise you are looking for!

Maybe you already have a name of a person or a company. That is already good information you can use to find the right people.

Strategy 2: Find More Experts

These are some additional strategies you can use to find more experts:

1. **Browse in the networks of the experts**. Chances are that they are connected with their colleagues in other departments in the same

country, affiliations in other countries and with their counterparts in other companies.

2. **Look in the Profile of experts at "Viewers of this Profile also viewed"**: in this way you might find other experts. You can find this at the right hand side at the bottom of someone's Profile.

3. **Join the Groups where the experts are a member of.** Look in the Profile of your connections; the Groups are at the bottom. In Groups you can also find people who are not in your first three degrees. An extra advantage of being a member of the same Group is that you are able to contact them directly (many people turn the general option of being open for direct contacts on LinkedIn off, but not in the Groups they are a member of).

4. **Look in "Companies" in the top menu of every page**. This might give you additional information about the organizations the experts are working for. Not all companies are in this directory, however, only the larger ones. It will also help you to discover divisions of that company. In this fast changing world we don't always know which company bought which (part of) another company.

Strategy 3: Look up the Experts on LinkedIn

Using the information from steps 1 and 2 you can do a search like we described in the previous chapter and ask the mutual connection to connect you with the expert via a Magic Email.

But what do you do after the connection is made?

Remember that the power of networking is in the second degree. So don't only focus on the person you have found, but also ask for introductions to other people.

Strategy 4: Join Groups

After defining the experts you are looking for it becomes much easier to choose which associations to join in real life. And also which Groups to join on LinkedIn.

You can search for Groups in the Groups Directory.

If you still don't know which Groups to join or which Groups the experts might be a member of, tap into the intelligence of LinkedIn: look in the Profile of the experts you are already connected to which Groups they are a member of. You might be surprised!

Once you are a member of a Group, remember it is about building relationships and increasing your own visibility and credibility. You can do this by contributing in the Discussion forums. Again, remember the forums are a place to help people and to give them advice. When giving advice and help, your know, like and trust factor will increase.

Other interesting Groups to join are Groups of people with the same function as yours. Not only can you learn from each other, but also they might connect you with the experts you are looking for.

Strategy 5: Answer Questions

Another way of increasing your visibility and credibility is answering questions in the Answer section of LinkedIn. You can make yourself stand out by the quality of your answers in the first place.

If the people who are asking questions consider you as the one with the best answer, they can also award you expert points. Depending on the category you are answering questions in this can quickly lead to extra visibility when you are on the Expert list.

A small note: at the time of writing there were only topic related categories. This means there was no connection with a specific geographic location or industry. So it depends on where your target group is and how active it is related to Answers whether it is worth your while or not.

Strategy 6: Increase your Number of Recommendations

As we said in Fundamental Principle Number 5: people do business with and refer business to people they know, like and trust.

What is interesting about trust is that it can be passed on. Or at least part of it. When you are looking for a plumber and a good friend of yours recommends one, don't you trust this person more?

LinkedIn also helps with that part: people can write Recommendations for each other. However, we are all so busy that most of us don't think about doing this spontaneously.

So how can you get more Recommendations? These are two strategies I suggest:

1. **Ask your current and past colleagues and other people you have worked with for a Recommendation**. You can use the tools that LinkedIn provides, but I would suggest adding at least some

other form of communication. In a face-to-face meeting or via the telephone bring up the Recommendations function of LinkedIn and ask them if they want to write a small Recommendation for you. Do this especially with past colleagues and other people you have worked with. For colleagues you can work with an email. Then you can send a reminder via LinkedIn in which you refer to your prior communication. You can do this under "Profile", "Recommendations" and then "Request Recommendation". Again, don't use the standard request, but make it personal and refer in the text to your meeting or call. This way of working is more time intensive then using the standard LinkedIn message, but the results will also be much better. Keep in mind that only using the standard LinkedIn message to request a Recommendation without any other communication might put off the people you want to write a Recommendation. The result will be then the opposite of you want to achieve: you will harm your relationships with your current contacts more than appearing more interesting for potential new contacts.

2. **Write a Recommendation for someone else first**. The standard message of LinkedIn after you have recommended someone (which you can't change) is an invitation to write a Recommendation for the person who just recommended you. Many people will do this. If you follow this strategy, always be honest and do not overly praise people you met only once. Then your chances to get a Recommendation back decrease. And if someone asks you later about this person you have to admit you don't know this person very well. This might harm your credibility with the third party.

Remarks:

- If you are not completely happy with the Recommendation because it is not accurate or too vague, you can ask them to modify the Recommendation. If after a modification you are still not happy, you can always choose not to show it on your Profile.

- Sometimes your contacts will reply that they don't know what to write. Then suggest you make a draft version that they can use to start from. If you are honest and don't exaggerate they will probably just post your draft version without changing anything.

Strategy 7: Use the "Status Update" function

The "Status Update" function allows you to share what you are doing right now. You have 100 characters.

How could this help you? If you are looking for a certain person, function or expertise you don't find on LinkedIn, you can mention this. This message is then shown to some or all people from your network. They might think of someone they know who is not on LinkedIn or who's Profile didn't match your search criteria.

You can choose who can see this "Status update": only your direct connections, your first three degrees or everyone. Depending on what you have written and who is in your network, you might change this every time you update your status.

Don't have too many expectations from this, not everybody reads these status updates and reacts on them. On the other hand, it only takes you a few seconds of your time and you never know who might help you.

Where to find this? Click in the left menu on "Profile", then in the white box under your picture you can update your status.

Remark: if you also have an account on other websites like Plaxo, Facebook, MySpace or Twitter, there are now tools, which have you, update your status on all websites at the same time. See chapter "Free Tools to save you time when working with LinkedIn".

Strategy 8: Watch the Network Updates

The Network Updates on your LinkedIn Home Page might give you interesting information.

For example, when someone changes position, changes companies or updates his Profile. After taking a course or completing a project someone might suddenly have the expertise or information you are looking for.

It is also interesting to see who joins the Groups you are a member of. This person might be new to LinkedIn and not connected to your network. So you won't be able to connect with them via your LinkedIn network. But you can connect with him via the Group.

See who is asking questions. And also who is answering them. This might give you information about specific situations at certain organizations or general tendencies in the marketplace.

Finally, it might also be interesting to see who is connecting to whom. If you suddenly see that an expert you weren't able to reach and a good business contact are connected, you might ask your contact introduce you (or even recommend you) to this expert.

Strategy 9: Create Alerts

LinkedIn offers the possibility to save your searches and run them automatically for you. In the free account there are 3 saved search slots. You can run them manually or have them run automatically every week or month.

Why can this be useful for you? After you have made a definition of the expert(s) and have experimented with the search function to find them, you can save this search and have it automatically run by LinkedIn. Every week or month LinkedIn will email you the new people who match the criteria in your saved search.

9 Advanced Strategies for Members of a Referral or Network Club

If you are in sales or have your own company and you are already a member of BNI, BRE, LeTip, BOB, Flevum, Netpluswork or any other referral club: well done, you are on your way to success!

Now let's see how LinkedIn can help you to get more out of your membership. The tips in this part are very similar to the ones finding a new customer, but tweaked to "educating" the people from your referral group so you can help them to help you better. Make sure you also read and apply the Advanced Strategies to find a new customer!

Strategy 1: Make a Good Profile and Connect with Every Member of your Referral Group

This might seem an obvious step, but many times we don't make a good Profile and we aren't connected to all the other members from our own group. We miss many opportunities to help them and to get help from them in that way.

When making a Profile on LinkedIn it should make clear for everybody and especially the members of your referral group, what you do.

It is also important to connect with all the other members so you can see who they are connected to (and who might be a good prospect for you) and give them the opportunity to see who you can refer them to.

Some people from your referral group won't have a Profile on LinkedIn yet. Offer to help them to make a Profile and to get started. Or organize a session for a few people at the same time.

Also add extra value to newcomers by inviting them to LinkedIn. If a new member gets 20 invitations to connect on LinkedIn after the first meeting, he might already experience what the power of this group (and the network behind this group) might be, making him wanting to come back and keep coming back!

Strategy 2: Make a Definition of Your Customer/Prospect

To receive good referrals, the first step to take is setting goals like we did in the previous chapter. Normally when defining a sales goal you will also make a good definition of people who are good prospects for you.

This is a crucial, but too many times overlooked step. Not defining (and updating!) a good definition of a prospect is what keeps the referrals from flowing. If you don't have a good definition, the members of your referral group don't know how they can help you. Or they give you the wrong referrals, which lead to a waste of time and frustration for all involved parties.

Take these things into account when you make a definition: what type of industry are they in? Which geographic location? Which functions or titles do the people you have contact with? Which other parameters do you have?

Maybe you already have a name of a person or a company from your prospect list. That is already good information you can use to help your referral group members to find the right people for you.

Strategy 3: Look in the Network of other Members to Find Prospects

Many times our fellow members could give us a good referral, but they don't know it themselves. They might be connected to people who might be a good prospect, but they never think of them when they think about our products or services.

This is where the power of LinkedIn can help you. By looking for prospects you might discover that someone from your referral group knows both of you. LinkedIn makes these connections visible.

The first strategy to find more prospects your referral group colleagues can introduce you to is browsing their network. Chances are that they are connected with potential customers.

Strategy 4: Look your Prospects up on LinkedIn

Using the definition from strategy 2 you can do a search like we described in the previous chapter. You might find out that one of your fellow referral group members knows the prospect.

You can then ask him to connect you with your prospect via a Magic Email.

But what do you do after the connection is made?

Remember that LinkedIn is a NETWORK platform and not a SALES platform.

This means that after you have received an introduction to a prospect you have to start building a relationship with them, not bombard them with sales calls and brochures.

So think about how you can help them. Think about what you can give or share with them without expecting anything in return without crossing your own boundaries. (For a list of things you can offer to other people I refer you to my book, "Let's Connect!")

Strategy 5: Increase your Number of Recommendations

As we said in Fundamental Principle Number 5: people do business with and refer business to people they know, like and trust.

What is interesting about trust is that it can be passed on. Or at least part of it. When you are looking for a plumber and a good friend of yours recommends one, don't you trust this person more?

LinkedIn also helps with that part: people can write Recommendations for each other. However, we are all so busy that most of us don't think about doing this spontaneously.

So how can you improve your Trust factor in your referral group and get more Recommendations? These are two strategies I suggest:

1. **Ask your current referral group colleagues for a Recommendation**. You can use the tools that LinkedIn provides, but I would suggest adding at least some other form of communication. In a face-to-face meeting or via the telephone bring up the Recommendations function of LinkedIn and ask them if they want to write a small Recommendation for you.
I strongly suggest you only ask people who had a (positive) experience with you for a Recommendation. Don't ask newcomers to the group for a Recommendation. They might feel obliged and

have a negative feeling about it. The result is the opposite effect of what you want to achieve!

Then you can send a reminder via LinkedIn in which you refer to your prior communication. You can do this under "Profile", "Recommendations" and then "Request Recommendation". Again, don't use the standard request, but make it personal and refer in the text to your meeting or call. This way of working is more time intensive then using the standard LinkedIn message, but the results will also be much better. Keep in mind that only using the standard LinkedIn message to request a Recommendation without any other communication might put off the people you want to write a Recommendation. The result will then be the opposite of what you want to achieve: you will harm your relationships with your current customers and colleagues more than appearing more interesting for potential customers.

2. **Write a Recommendation for someone else first**. The standard message of LinkedIn after you have recommended someone (which you can't change) is an invitation to write a Recommendation for the person who just recommended you. Many people will do this. If you follow this strategy, always be honest and do not overly praise people you met only once. Then your chances to get a Recommendation back decrease. And if someone asks you later about this person you have to admit you don't know this person very well. This might harm your credibility with the third party.

Remarks:

- If you are not completely happy with the Recommendation because it is not accurate or too vague, you can ask them to modify the Recommendation. If after a modification you are still not happy, you can always choose not to show it on your Profile.

- Sometimes your contacts will reply that they don't know what to write. Then suggest you make a draft version that they can use to start from. If you are honest and don't exaggerate they will probably just post your draft version without changing anything.

Strategy 6: Watch the Network Updates

The Network Updates on your LinkedIn Home Page might give you interesting information.

For example, when you see a colleague from your referral group connecting to a prospect. As you see this happening you might ask your colleague to introduce you (or even recommend you) to this prospect.

Strategy 7: Make a Group on LinkedIn

When you are responsible for the local chapter of the referral organization you are a member of, you might consider starting a Group on LinkedIn. Especially when you don't have any other online group or online presence (see also the next part about Advanced Strategies for Organizations and Group Managers).

This can be a spot where members can give each other advice and tips and where they can ask for help. This might be a valuable extra to your face-to-face meetings.

Strategy 8: Answer Questions in the Discussions of your Group

If your referral group has a Group on LinkedIn (or on another website), this is an excellent place to show yourself to the other members.

How to do this? Don't promote yourself (unless this is explicitly encouraged by the Group Manager), but look for ways you can help your fellow members.

By answering the questions they have and providing good help you increase your visibility and credibility. Also share the positive comments you hear from the contacts you introduced a fellow referral group member to. Honest public praise always works very well. It works even more online because it is written down instead of spoken out loud (but also keep doing that!). Also invite your contact to write a Recommendation on LinkedIn for your referral group colleague.

As a consequence of you being active in the LinkedIn Group your Like and Trust factor will increase and your referral group colleagues will have a higher esteem of you and give you more referrals.

Strategy 9: Attend Every Meeting of your Referral Group to Reinforce your LinkedIn Efforts

By now you already understand how LinkedIn can add to the results you get from your referral group membership.

It also works the other way around: by attending the meetings of your referral group, you will add to the actions you take on LinkedIn.

These are the benefits of attending the meetings:

- When attending meetings you can (and should!) **give examples** of projects you did for customers. This will help your colleagues think of extra contacts they have for you on LinkedIn and in other networks. Even when you have a good Profile, there is no room for examples or stories (you might want to add them, but that could make your Profile unattractive to read).

- After discovering that a fellow referral group member is in contact with a prospect, you can **talk before or after a meeting about how well they know each other, give more background about a request and suggest the best way to refer you**. This will help him to give you a better referral and you get a better result.

- It is **easier for people to get to know, like and trust each other when they meet each other face-to-face**. They can experience how the other person behaves towards them and towards the other members.

As you see, a membership of a referral organization combined with a (pro) active presence on LinkedIn is a killer combination to get referral after referral.

If you want even more tips on how to build an effective referral strategy, take a look at our Everlasting Referrals Home Study Course: www.everlasting-referrals.com

12 Advanced Strategies for Organizations or Group Managers

It pays off for people who are in charge of a (professional) organization to have a LinkedIn Group. It might stimulate the interactions between the members and increase the amount of members in the "real life" organization.

Here are some advanced strategies to build your LinkedIn Group.

Strategy 1: Make a Definition of the type of members you want

To attract the right members, the first step to take is setting goals like we did in the previous chapter. Normally when defining that goal you will also make a good definition of the members you are looking for.

Take these things into account: what type of industry? Which geographic location? Which functions or titles are you focusing on? Which other parameters do you have? Remember to use several synonyms of the function you are looking for!

Strategy 2: Create a Group, invite your current members and make some rules

To start working online with your organization create a Group on LinkedIn and invite the current members of your organization. If you have a database or Excel sheet with names and email addresses of your members, you should be able to do this in 15 minutes.

In the invitation message explain the benefits of joining this Group for them. Also ask them to show the logo of your LinkedIn Group in their Profile (If they still don't see why they should use LinkedIn and become a member, buy them this book ☺)

It is also important to create some rules for the interactions in the Group. The Discussions sections in some Groups get cluttered with messages, which are not relevant or are shameless sales pitches. When you have defined some rules all members have to play by, it is easier to prevent this behavior or take action when it happens.

Having this online presence as a LinkedIn Group will attract potential new members. They might never have heard of your organization, but by searching for Groups or by looking in the Profiles of their contacts they might stumble upon your LinkedIn Group.

Strategy 3: Add value to the LinkedIn Group

Many forums and clubs online get a good start, but "die" after a few months. The reason is that in the beginning it is new and there are some interactions, but after a while the initial momentum fades away and the forum is not used anymore.

Be aware of the 1-9-90 rule. This means that in normal forums 1% of the members is very proactive, 9% of the members reacts on the 1% and 90% just watches or isn't active at all.

However, you can do something about it. As a Group Manager (or preferably a team of Group Managers) you can stimulate interaction in several ways:

1. Post interesting articles in the News section.

2. Post questions in the Discussions yourself.

3. Answer questions in the Discussions yourself.

4. Post a preview for the next event or a review from a past event.

5. Ask an expert from the Group or external to the Group to write an article and then post it in the News section.

6. Send messages to members who might be the expert with an invitation to respond to a question, but haven't read the question.

7. If you want to stimulate (immediate) interaction it might be a good idea to send messages to a few people asking them to join the discussion. Why? Many people have set their notifications for new postings on "weekly". However, don't overdo it and only do this when the discussion topic is really interesting.

8. Post in the Discussions the name of the expert who might be the solution. Public praise is always appreciated.

9. Avoid clutter in the Discussions section. When members post messages that are not "accepted" according to the rules you have set up, you can point out that the Discussions is not the place for this kind of messages. Keep in mind that most people who post "inappropriate" messages most of the time don't know how to interact in forums. Help them. Removing these messages and replacing them with "good ones" will also help keep the other members happy.

10. Be a matchmaker between members. When you meet someone online or off-line who might be interesting for another member, connect the two with each other. This action alone will create a happy community of members who will keep extending their membership year after year.

11. Extra action for outside the Group: suggest your members as experts in the Answers section.

Strategy 4: Use the free LinkedIn Group to attract more members

Most professional organizations' focus is on events and meetings where people can meet each other face-to-face. This is still the best way to get in touch with people and to maintain the relationships with your current contacts. If done well people also want to pay for that.

Adding a LinkedIn Group (or another online forum) will certainly help current members to find each other, keep in touch and get introduced to each other's connections. This alone should be the reason to start a LinkedIn Group.

Some organizations might also want to charge for this online interaction or include it in the business model. And that can be a good solution.

Other organizations want to grow the amount of members. A good strategy can then be to have an open and free LinkedIn Group to attract more potential members. Benefits of this strategy:

- Potential members can get a taste of why the organization might be an interesting one to join. If you follow strategy 3 this will become very clear to them very quickly.

- The more people in the LinkedIn Group (who bring their first and second degree network via their Profile with them) the more interesting the Group will become for the current members. This will also help to retain current members.

Be aware that only few people know all the benefits of LinkedIn and the LinkedIn Groups. That's why I wrote this book, to help them to understand these benefits. So it is important to help the members of your Group to get started. After reading this book you will have enough ideas to do that. However if you need some extra help, contact us at connect-with-us@ networking-coach.com.

Strategy 5: Ask the members to invite their contacts

If you want to grow your organization you can ask current members of your organization to become a member of your LinkedIn Group and show your LinkedIn Group logo in their Profile. This will attract a few people.

The next step is to ask them to invite people from their network to become a member as well. To have good interactions and a feeling of "quality" be sure to mention once again the type of people you want in the Group.

They will be much more inclined to do this if they feel the value of being a member of this Group themselves. Applying strategy 3 will ensure they will have experienced the value.

Strategy 6: Look for potential members yourself and ask current members to help

Despite the fact you might have provided good value to the members of the Group, still some people won't invite other people who might be interested in and interesting for the Group. The main reason: they don't take the time to think of who might be interested in joining the Group.

What you can do in that situation is help them to help you.

You can use these strategies:

- Use the parameters of the definition you have made in strategy 1 to do a search. Then you will see which current member is connected to the potential member.

- Browse in the connections of your current members to see if you can find potential members.

- Look in the Profile of current and potential members at "Viewers of this Profile also viewed" for other potential members. You can find this feature at the right hand side at the bottom of someone's Profile.

Then ask the current member to invite this particular member. Sending an email is the least time consuming. If people don't know what to write provide them with a draft text they can use to invite their contact.

Of course if current members haven't experienced any value from their membership of the organization or the LinkedIn Group they will be reluctant to do this. So make sure you apply strategy 3 first.

Strategy 7: Increase your Number of Recommendations

As we said in Fundamental Principle Number 5: people do business with and refer business to people they know, like and trust.

What is interesting about trust is that it can be passed on. Or at least part of it. When you are looking for a plumber and a good friend of yours recommends one, don't you trust this person more?

LinkedIn also helps with that part: people can write Recommendations for each other. However, we are all so busy that most of us don't think about doing this spontaneously.

Especially if you want to attract more potential members it is important to have some Recommendations from current members.

So how can you get more Recommendations? These are two strategies I suggest:

1. **Ask your current members for a Recommendation**. You can use the tools that LinkedIn provides, but I would suggest adding at least some other form of communication. In a face-to-face meeting or via the telephone bring up the Recommendations function of LinkedIn and ask them if they want to write a small Recommendation for you.

Then you can send a reminder via LinkedIn in which you refer to your prior communication. You can do this under "Profile", "Recommendations" and then "Request Recommendation". Again, don't use the standard request, but make it personal and refer in the text to your meeting or call. This way of working is more time intensive then using the standard LinkedIn message, but the results will also be much better. Keep in mind that only using the standard LinkedIn message to request a Recommendation without any other communication might put off the people you want to write a Recommendation. The result will then be the opposite of you want to achieve: you will harm your relationships with your current contacts more than appearing more interesting for potential members.

2. **Write a Recommendation for someone else first**. The standard message of LinkedIn after you have recommended someone (which you can't change) is an invitation to write a Recommendation for the person who just recommended you. Many people will do this. If you follow this strategy, always be honest and do not overly praise people you met only once. Then your chances to get a Recommendation back decrease. And if someone asks you later about this person you have to admit you don't know this person very well. This might harm your credibility with the third party.

Remarks:

- If you are not completely happy with the Recommendation because it is not accurate or too vague, you can ask them to modify the Recommendation. If after a modification you are still not happy, you can always choose not to show it on your Profile.

- Sometimes your contacts will reply that they don't know what to write. Then suggest you make a draft version that they can use to start from. If you are honest and don't exaggerate they will probably just post your draft version without changing anything.

Strategy 8: Use the "Status Update" function

The "Status Update" function allows you to share what you are doing right now. You have 100 characters.

How could this help you? When your next event is due or if you are looking for a certain person or function you don't find on LinkedIn, you can mention this. This message is then shown to some or all people from your network. They might think of someone they know who is not on LinkedIn or who's Profile didn't match your search criteria.

You can choose who can see this "Status update": only your direct connections, your first three degrees or everyone. Depending on what you have written and who is in your network, you might change this every time you update your status.

Don't have too many expectations from this, not everybody reads these status updates and reacts on them. On the other hand, it only takes you a few seconds of your time and you never know who might help you.

Where to find this? Click in the left menu on "Profile", then in the white box under your picture you can update your status.

Remark: if you also have an account on other websites like Plaxo, Facebook, MySpace or Twitter, there are now tools, which have you, update your status on all websites at the same time. See chapter "Free Tools to save you time when working with LinkedIn".

Strategy 9: Watch the Network Updates

The Network Updates on your LinkedIn Home Page might give you interesting information.

For example, when one of the current members is connecting with a potential member. You might ask the current member to invite the potential member to the LinkedIn Group or introduce you to the new member.

Other interesting information is when a current member has a new position. This might mean he might not qualify as a member anymore, but his replacement might. Inquire about the situation and ask for an introduction to the new person.

Strategy 10: Use LinkedIn as a potential member generator by creating alerts

LinkedIn offers the possibility to save your searches and run them automatically for you. In the free account there are 3 saved search slots. You can run them manually or have them run automatically every week or month.

Why can this be useful for you? After you have made a definition of what the type of members is that you want and have experimented with the search function to find them, you can save this search and have it automatically run by LinkedIn. Every week or month LinkedIn will email you the new people who match the criteria in your saved search.

Strategy 11: Find Speakers or Guest Editors

Most organizations need speakers for their events or guest editors for their magazine or website on a continuous basis. For some organizers it is easy to find them, but for many organizers after a while it becomes harder and it takes more time to find speakers or guest editors (and they can't keep inviting someone from our team at Networking Coach for every event ☺)

These are a few strategies to use LinkedIn to find a speaker or guest editor:

- **Post this question in the Discussions of your own LinkedIn Group**. Make sure you are specific enough otherwise you will receive many suggestions which will cost you time to investigate, but won't produce any results.

- **Post this question in the Discussions of one of the LinkedIn Groups for speakers**. Use the "Find a Group" function in the Groups Directory. If you don't want to become a member of that Group, ask the Group Manager to post this question for you.

- **Use the "Advanced Search" with the right parameters to find them**. Get connected via a Magic Email or via "Get Introduced Through a Connection".

- **Browse in the connections of a speaker you hired in the past**. Of course you can always contact him with your question. Get connected via a Magic Email or via "Get Introduced Through a Connection".

If you still don't find a speaker, look at the website of the International Federation for Professional Speakers (http://www.iffps.org/) At the bottom of the home page there are also links to the websites of the Professional Speakers organizations in the member countries with local speakers. You can also send us an email at connect-with-us@networking-coach.com with the kind of speaker you are looking for and we will see with whom we can get you connected.

Strategy 12: use Events to promote your events

A relatively new feature on LinkedIn is the Events. You can post an event and people can tell whether they are coming or not. They can also share it with up to 50 of their LinkedIn contacts in one message. You can also create a LinkedIn Ad for the event. (Note: at the moment of writing this functionality is only available for US Profiles).

Using this functionality you might get more attendants than when only using your normal channels.

At the moment of writing this feature is only accessible via the Home Page and not very visible. So don't expect too many people finding your event without a little help from your network.

But just putting your event in the calendar is free, so why wouldn't you take 3 minutes to do it?

How to add an Event to the calendar?

- Go to "Applications" on the left hand menu.
- Click on the + sign.
- Click on "Events".
- At the top of the new page, click on "Add Event"

Conclusion of this chapter

By now you not only have a basic strategy about how to grow your network on LinkedIn and how to really tap into the power of your network, but also various advanced strategies related to task(s) you need to do.

Whether you are looking for new customers, a new job or internship, new employees, suppliers, partners or internal/external expertise, there are many advanced strategies for you. Also for members of referral or network clubs and people who are responsible for professional organizations and associations there are advanced strategies.

Some of these advanced strategies are: making a definition of the type of people you are looking for, how to find them via using the Search function, browsing in the networks of your contacts, finding Groups via the Profile of your contacts, answering questions in Groups and Answers, giving and receiving Recommendations, notifying your network via Status Update and getting notifications via Network Updates and creating Alerts.

To be really successful and to avoid some pitfalls while using LinkedIn it is recommended to know about some hot discussions topics and specific behavior of LinkedIn. You also might want to reduce the time you invest when using LinkedIn. So I advise you to read the last 3 chapters as well, apply the tips you get there and use the free tools to help you save time.

Answers to Hot Discussion Topics and Burning Questions

Since we receive lots of questions about following or not following certain strategies, I have listed in this chapter some of the topics that always lead to discussions. You will also get answers to frequently asked questions.

Sometimes I will give you direct advice; sometimes I will just show you both sides of a discussion.

Not everybody is on LinkedIn so it doesn't work

A comment we hear often is: "Not every person or every function is on LinkedIn. I can't always find the right person. LinkedIn doesn't work for me." It is right that not everybody is a member of LinkedIn. But the network is growing VERY fast. From 19 million to 32 million users worldwide in one year (2008) is a fast growing pace. So maybe the person you are looking for was not on LinkedIn yesterday, but signed up today.

Let's also look at it from another perspective: a few years ago, when LinkedIn didn't exist, it was almost impossible to find the paths between people. Or it cost lots of time. Now LinkedIn makes it a lot easier. And if you don't find the person you are looking for, what keeps you from doing it "the old way"?

I repeat what I wrote before. Despite the fact that not every person is on LinkedIn, it is a website for business networking. What we see in practice is that the majority of organizations are represented on LinkedIn (In the USA, all of the Fortune 500 companies have an executive level presence). Maybe you won't find the Marketing Manager of a company, but you might find the IT Manager. The Marketing Manager is only one step away from him. OK, it is some extra effort, but still lots easier than before LinkedIn existed.

No one has contacted me yet. So LinkedIn is a useless business tool.

On the contrary! LinkedIn is a super tool, which helps you to find the people who are in the best position to help you reach your goals, whatever they may be.

However, many people think that if they make a Profile other people will contact them. When I ask the people who complain about this if they ever contacted someone themselves almost all of them remain silent.

Does that mean that LinkedIn doesn't work? No! If you use the strategies explained in this book to proactively use LinkedIn, it can quickly bring you new customers, a new job, new employees, suppliers, partners, expertise,...

Remember that if you want to see some results, you are responsible for them. You have to take action. And LinkedIn is a great tool to support you.

I am happy with my current professional situation, why should I build a network on LinkedIn (or elsewhere)?

Let me start by answering you don't have to do anything. All the tips in this book are suggestions and tips that are derived from my experience with giving hundreds of training courses and presentations about networking or referrals and from using LinkedIn myself.

So why build a network on LinkedIn? For starters almost everybody needs some expert advice once in a while or new connections inside or outside a company. LinkedIn helps you to find these experts and the people who can introduce you to them. So that is one reason.

The second and maybe even more important reason is that I see too many people only start building their network when it is too late. People who got unexpectedly fired and needed to find a new job suddenly realized they needed a network to help them. Then they get on LinkedIn and start building their network, which takes time. Many times time they don't have.

The same applies to entrepreneurs. I meet so many people who have a great idea, leave their job, start a company, invest a lot of money and after a few months they realize they also need customers. And a lot. And fast. Why? Because the monthly costs and investments are high. Then they realize they need to start building their network while they should have done that months ago.

In these two examples they start building the network when they NEED it URGENTLY. This creates an energy of despair, which turns people off instead of making them interested to help you.

So start building your network before you actually need it. You can then interact in a normal way with the networking attitude of sharing without expecting anything immediately in return.

Why would I use LinkedIn if I can use Google to find information?

Google is an excellent resource to find information. So use it when you look for **information**.

LinkedIn is a collection of people and the relationships between them. Use LinkedIn when you are looking for a **person**.

People with thousands of connections

Some people on LinkedIn have tens of thousands of contacts. Most of the time they call themselves LIONS, which is an abbreviation of LinkedIn Open Networkers. They are open to anyone who wants to connect with them and they also actively connect with as many people as possible.

Since LinkedIn shows the amount of people you have in your network up to 500, many of them will list in their description how many connections they actually have.

Many times we hear in our presentations and training courses: "These people are only focused on collecting people (like stamps), they are not looking for real connections". Some of the participants then say they only want to connect with people they know very well and who they are willing to recommend.

The LIONS themselves say that having so many connections helps them to connect with many people to reach their goals and that they are also able to help people from their network better when they have so many connections.

Personally my own approach lies in between both approaches. This discussion also goes back to the quality-diversity topic that I addressed in the first chapter.

For me I connect with people:

- When I have met them personally in real life.
- Or when they send me a personal message with a good reason why they want to connect with me.

So does that mean I connect with everybody? No, so I'm not a LION. On the other hand I acknowledge there is value in having a large network. But for me there still has to be a personal contact moment. Does that mean that I'm willing to recommend all of them? No! Only when I've had a personal experience with them will I write a Recommendation for them.

So what is my advice to you? To do like me? No. I wanted to share the different perspectives so you can make a better choice yourself.

Hide or show my connections?

On the "Account & Settings" page under "Privacy Settings/Connections Browse" you can turn off the option that other people can browse through your network from your Profile.

Sometimes people have their reasons not to be willing to show their network. I always ask the question: what do you expect from the other people on LinkedIn? Do you expect them to open their network for you, but you don't want to do it for them? Doesn't seem a fair deal to me.

If you don't allow your network to see your connections and also don't expect them to share their connections with yours, then it is something else.

Some people don't want others to browse through their connections because they don't want their competitors to see which customers they have. For me this is not a solution. If you fear that someone might "steal" your customers because they see the connections on LinkedIn, then you better work on your relationship with your customer. Happy customers don't switch, even neutral ones not always. Why? Because change brings uncertainties. In most cases people like to stay where they are and especially when they get a product/ service of a good quality for a reasonable price.

By the way if you use the search function and find someone who is in the network of a contact who has turned the "Connections Browse" off, both will still appear in the list.

Block access to LinkedIn for employees?

Some organizations are blocking websites like LinkedIn because they fear that their employees will get job offers from other companies. Others do it because their employees spend too much time on LinkedIn and other websites.

Is blocking the websites a good idea? Not in my opinion.

For organizations, which fear their employees might leave because someone contacts them, I have the same remark as for people who fear their competitors might "steal" their customers because they know of the connections. If people are happy, they won't leave a company. So make sure they are happy and feel respected. Then you don't have anything to fear. If they are not happy and you block LinkedIn, they will use it at home on their own time. However, the result will be the same.

For organizations which fear that their employees are wasting their time on LinkedIn instead of being productive I have the following advice: instead of blocking websites teach people how to use them to save time and get better results faster. And if necessary, make a policy so everybody is clear about this situation.

Blocking websites like LinkedIn doesn't make much sense in today's world where everybody and everything is connected. Social networks are the tools of the young generations. They are using them and will keep using them. There is no stopping them from doing that in their spare time. Instead of fighting against these technologies it makes more sense to use them to your own advantage.

When should I start building my network?

The answer is simple: now! Many people only start building or maintaining their network when they need a job, a customer or something else. And most of the time when they need it very bad and very fast. As a consequence, they are under such time pressure that they want to bypass the fundamental principles of networking. However, the result is that people react negatively towards this kind of behavior, which makes them even more "desperate", bypassing the principles even more and get in a downward spiral.

So start building your network now when you don't have the time pressure. Apply the fundamental principles and enjoy the process.

How much time do I have to spend on LinkedIn?

Since we all are different people, have different personalities and have different goals, this is a hard question to answer.

Some people just love to be connected the whole time via all kind of tools like telephone, email, online networking and instant messaging. Others like to work alone or have a quiet time alone in the evenings and weekends.

There are also moments in your life where you want or need more interaction than other times.

That being said, what I advise you to do is to invest time to apply the basic strategy, do the GAIN exercise for one goal on paper and then use the advanced strategy that fits your situation the most to experience how LinkedIn can help you.

Afterwards it is your own choice how much time you allocate to work with LinkedIn.

What I suggest as a minimum time allocation when you are not actively working on a goal (let's call it maintenance) is spend one hour a week to look at the Discussions of the Groups you are a member of and contribute to them, look at the Network Updates from your network and also see if you could connect some people with each other or can help someone who asked a question in Answers.

Next to a daily or weekly update from what is going on in your Groups I also suggest you have personal messages delivered immediately so you won't miss out on an opportunity. When people are looking for someone or something they nowadays don't have the time to wait a week for an answer.

Can I only connect with people I know very well? If I connect with others I can't recommend them.

It is very important to keep the difference between an introduction and a recommendation in mind. You can only honestly recommend people you have had an experience with. But don't let that keep you from making introductions. You can always introduce two people to each other without even knowing them well. However, the words you use when you make the introduction are important.

If you only met someone for 5 minutes, but think that he might be of help to one of your business contacts use a phrase like: "HI Marie, I want to introduce you to John Smith. I met John at the Safety conference last week. In the 5 minutes we were able to speak to each other he told me he just finished doing a safety project at a large chemical plant. Maybe he can help you too with your projects."

When you use words like "last week, 5 minutes and maybe" Marie will know that you don't have any personal experience with John and that you can't recommend him. But she will be happy that you thought of her and wanted to help her.

When is a relationship good enough to send someone an invitation? And how to do that?

There is no number of meetings or number of hours you talked to someone you can use as an indicator. Sometimes you can send an invitation after one conversation; sometimes you will never send one.

For me the indicator is how the conversation went. Did you have something in common? Was there a "click"? Bringing up LinkedIn in a conversation also helps to speed up the process. You can then hear whether this person uses LinkedIn or not and how he feels about receiving invitations.

The best way to bring it up is when you have focused in the conversation on what you could do for the other person or who you could connect him to. Then it is easy to say: "Is it OK that I send you an invitation on LinkedIn so you will be immediately connected via me with the person we were talking about?"

One other tip: look always how you can help someone else or how you can be of added value to someone. Many times it is via our network.

I have many contacts from years ago. Can I still contact them?

Yes, you can always reconnect with them. Don't feel bad that it is from such a long time ago. They didn't take action either. They probably have the same hesitation as you do.

When you reconnect with them, always make your message personal. Refer to the time you spent together, the projects you worked on or the time in college. Use the name in your invitation message you were known by the time you knew them. This especially applies to women who now go by the name of their husband.

What to do with an invitation from someone I don't know very well?

Of course it depends on what your own strategy on LinkedIn is and the nature of the invitation. But let's assume you don't really want to be connected. There are three strategies you can follow:

1. Do nothing. Don't accept, don't push on "I Don't Know this person" and don't reply.

2. Use the "reply" button to explain you only connect with people you know very well.

3. Accept the invitation. Then later use "Remove Connections". This person won't be notified of this action.

How to deal with invitations from people I don't know at all (or think I don't know)?

The biggest problem with LinkedIn is that many people don't know they can personalize the invitation message or that they don't see a good reason why they should do this.

I hope you understand by now that LinkedIn is a tool to build relationships. It is hard building relationships with impersonal messages. Next to that, an invitation is another contact moment you have with that particular person. So make your messages as personal as possible!

However, only a few people send a personalized invitation message. Personally I receive a lot of these messages. Since I meet many people sometimes I don't know if I have already met them or not. So I always reply to the invitation messages.

This is the message I use:

> HI xxx,
>
> Thank you for your invitation to connect!
>
> Unfortunately, I meet so many people that I can't always "put the name and face together".
>
> Can you help me by reminding me where we met?
>
> Thanks and ... have a great networking day!
>
> Jan

It then depends on the answer I get whether I accept the invitation or not. If I never hear from them again, then I don't take any further action myself either. If they are indeed able to refresh my memory or give me a good and personal reason to connect with me, I accept the invitation.

How to deal with requests for recommendations from people I don't really know?

One of the fears of people to connect with other people they don't have a personal relationship with is that they are going get requests to recommend them. And they don't want to give a recommendation because they don't have a personal experience with them.

What do you do when you are connected to someone you don't really know and he asks you for a recommendation?

This is a tip from Bob Burg, author of "Endless Referrals" and "The Go Giver":

I often talk about how to say "no" to a request that is either unreasonable or simply one you don't want to say "yes" to. The key is to do so in such a way that the other person is not offended and not made to feel shamed for asking, while at the same time not "leaving the door open" for them to come back with an answer to your "objection."

For example, on LinkedIn you can write a written "recommendation" for someone that will show up on their Profile page. Fine. Unfortunately, there are people who will ask you to do this when you have never experienced their work or even had any significant interchange with them.

Uncomfortable situation. How do you say "no" without causing them embarrassment (which will often turn into their blaming and resenting you) and in such a way that they will both understand and respect your decision? The following should work just fine:

> *HI xxx,*
>
> *Thank you so much for asking me to write a recommendation for you on LinkedIn. You seem like a great person and I'm sure your work is excellent. Of course, because I haven't experienced your work directly, it would be difficult for me to write a recommendation as though I have. But I truly do appreciate the fact that you thought highly enough of me to ask.*
>
> *Thank you for understanding. I have a feeling there are many people who have benefited from your fine work and will be delighted to provide a recommendation based on their actual experience with you.*
>
> *With best regards,*
>
> *Bob*

How do I ask a question to my whole network?

Option 1: use Answers

You can use "Answers" to ask a public question and/or 200 people from your first degree network. "Public" means that it will be posted in "Answers". Everybody can react on it. However, you can also choose to send it only to (up to 200 of) your contacts.

Here is how to do it (from the Help page of LinkedIn. If they already did a good job, why reinvent the wheel ☺):

- Click on "Answers" in the top navigation area of the top of the home page.

- Click on "Ask a Question".

- Type your question in the open text field.

- Below the question text field, you can select the "only share this question with connections I select". Use this only if you do not want your question posted publicly.

- Complete the provided form.

- Click on the "Ask Question" button at the bottom of the "Ask a Question" page.

- If you did not select the "share this question with connections" your answer will be posted publicly. You then have the option to select up to 200 connections you wish to send the question to and click on "Finished".

- Compose your email to your connections and click on "Send".

Option 2: compose a message

You can also send a message to people from your network. Per message you send you can add up to 50 people (it used to be only 10).

How do you do that?

- Go to "Inbox/Compose Message" in the left hand menu or to "Inbox" and then on the right hand side you see a button "Compose Message"

- To choose the recipients you have two options:

  - Start typing the first or last name of one of your first degree contacts and LinkedIn will present you with everybody whose name starts with the letters you have typed.

  - Click the "In" logo. Your list with Connections appears. Pick the Connections you want to send the message to.

Do I need to upgrade my membership?

Most people are just fine with a free account. However, if you are a heavy LinkedIn user who wants more than 5 introductions "en route" at the same time, wants to contact people directly via InMail or wants to be able to do reference searches, then you want to upgrade.

What do you get when you pay? On the next pages you will find an overview of the most interesting features.

Feature / Account Type	Personal	Business	Business Plus	Pro	My remarks and opinion
Send Requests for Introductions	5 at a time	15 at a time	25 at a time	40 at a time	Although this might be an appealing function, it is always better to have someone else send a Magic Email or send a normal message to you and the person you want to reach, because the action comes from someone you both know instead of by you.
Send InMails	No	3 per month	10 per month	50 per month	An InMail is direct message to someone who is not in your network and is not a member of the OpenLink network (see below). This is a way to directly reach people, but everybody can turn off the option that they can be contacted through InMail. Next to that an introduction via a mutual (trusted) contact always works better.
Receive OpenLink Messages	No	Unlimited	Unlimited	Unlimited	Everybody who has an upgraded account can choose to send and receive messages from other members with an upgraded account (then you are a member of the OpenLink network, sending messages is free). An extra advantage is that people who are outside your first, second and third degree can see your full Profile instead of a summary Profile. This might make sense for you if you want to increase your exposure and possibilities to interact with others. However, since you don't know who else has an upgraded account, the people you are looking for might not be amongst them. Use LinkedIn as a research database and then ask for a Magic Email. It will work better in most cases.

Feature / Account Type	Personal	Business	Business Plus	Pro	My remarks and opinion
Access to	First, second, third degree network and fellow Group members.	Whole LinkedIn network	Whole LinkedIn network	Whole LinkedIn network	Might be interesting for recruiters. However, for them and most other people it makes more sense to define their goals first and then expand their network in a particular direction using Introductions, Magic Emails and memberships of the right Groups. This strategy will normally ensure that you will be able to reach the people you are looking for via your first three degree network or in a Group.
Reference Searches	No	Yes	Yes	Yes	This is a valuable option if you want to check with some colleagues of someone you want to hire or form a business partnership with.
Search Results	100	300	500	700	In my opinion more than 100 search results only makes sense for sales people using LinkedIn for making a prospect list or for recruiters. Even then it makes sense to add extra search criteria to make the result group smaller to find the people in the best position to help you.
Saved Searches	Maximum 3, weekly alerts	Maximum 5, weekly alerts	Maximum 7, weekly alerts	Maximum 10, daily alerts	Saved Searches which are run automatically (alerts) are interesting in this way: when someone with a Profile that is interesting to you joins LinkedIn or changes jobs you are notified automatically. However, they are run only weekly so if you need to be "on the ball" only a Pro account will do the trick.

Feature / Account Type	Personal	Business	Business Plus	Pro	My remarks and opinion
Expanded LinkedIn Network Profiles	No	Yes	Yes	Yes	When you have an upgraded account you can see the expanded Profiles of everybody. Otherwise you can only see the expanded Profile of the people in your first, second and third degree network and of your fellow Group members.

My conclusion: at the time of writing it is not necessary for most people to upgrade their account.

You can find an overview of actual features and fees on the "Account & Settings" page.

If only a few people pay for their membership, where does LinkedIn get their money from?

Next to the venture capitalists that invested in the company, as far as I know LinkedIn gets money via these channels:

- Google Ads on the Profile pages
- LinkedIn Direct Ads (USA only for the moment)
- Job Postings
- Polls for a specific target group

By the way, in the FAQ pages LinkedIn says, "Joining LinkedIn is and will remain free." (Answer ID 55).

What is the number of connections I need to make LinkedIn work for me?

Of course it depends on the situation. Many contacts with people from the Telecom sector in Australia when you want to find a job in the Health sector in Budapest might be less ideal.

But let's assume you have followed the strategies in this book, then I can agree with Jason Alba who wrote in "I'm on LinkedIn, Now What?" that 60 connections should be enough to reach your goals via them and their network.

Why use a Group on LinkedIn instead of the Yahoo or PHP forums?

For me the biggest reason is that people are tired of visiting several websites to access all the communities they are a member of. So one website where they can consult their network of contacts and Groups make sense.

What also happens is that they think: "Since I just looked someone up on LinkedIn, I can also quickly look what is going on in the Groups I'm a member of" while they might not think of visiting the Yahoo or PHP forum.

Should I put my email address in my name?

This is a tactic that is applied by many LION's and other people who want to receive many invitations. So if that's what you want, you can do it. However, be warned that it is against the LinkedIn User Agreement. As far as I know, they haven't banned anyone for doing this, but they have the right to do so.

What is the value of Recommendations?

Since many people get Recommendations from friends and befriended co-workers who are not really objective or give rather vague Recommendations, people asked me what the value of their own carefully selected Recommendations is.

A few remarks:

- It is better to have a few Recommendations than no Recommendations.

- However, people who really value Recommendations will read them. If the Recommendations are vague and fluffy, they won't be taken into account.

- That's why it is important to ask for a modification of a Recommendation if you are not happy with it. Suggest the other person makes it more specific.

Conclusion of this chapter

In this chapter you have received the answers to many frequently asked questions in our training courses, presentations and webinars. I also shared my opinion about some hot discussion topics.

Think of this advice when using LinkedIn. Also come back to this chapter when you have a question yourself.

If you haven't found an answer to your question, look in the Help section of LinkedIn. That's also the place where I go when I have a question. You also might consult the "Answers" section on LinkedIn (subcategory Using LinkedIn). If you still haven't found an answer yet, you can always contact the LinkedIn Help Desk (also via the "Help" function).

Little known, but interesting features and behavior of LinkedIn

LinkedIn has many small and big features, which are not generally known. Or at least not many people know how they really work.

This chapter will give you more insights in those sometimes hidden gems, sometimes seemingly obvious options.

LinkedIn is a three degree network

It is important to know that LinkedIn considers only your first three degrees as your network. People you are connected with in the fourth degree or higher will appear as "out of your network". In one way this makes sense because the more degrees in between, the less personal the connections are and the harder it gets to reach them.

If you still want to reach people who are not in your network, become a member of a Group they are also a member of. Then you can contact them directly (if they didn't change the standard Group settings; what most people don't do).

Hidden connections can still be found

On the "Account & Settings" page under "Privacy Settings/Connections Browse" you can turn off the option that other people can browse through your network from your Profile.

However if someone uses the search function and finds one of your first degree contacts, this contact will still appear in the list of search results.

Direct contact still possible despite invitation filtering

On the "Account & Settings" page under "Email notifications/Invitation filtering" you can choose who is allowed to contact you:

1. All invitations (default).

2. Only invitations from people who know my email address or appear in my "Imported Contacts" list.

3. Only invitations from people who appear in my "Imported Contacts" list.

Some people choose option 2 or 3 so they will receive only invitations and messages from people they know.

However, they still can receive messages from people they don't know. From whom? From the members of the Groups they are a member of.

There is also an option to turn off to receive messages from other members, but standard this option is "on". You also have to change that for every Group you are a member of.

If you want to do that, go to "Groups", choose a Group, then under the tab "Settings" check off the Member Messages box "Allow members of this Group to send me messages via LinkedIn ".

You have lots of controls over the emails you receive through LinkedIn and your overall user experience

LinkedIn offers many options whether to receive invitations from people or not, to receive daily or weekly emails, or to personalize your Home Page,...

The majority of these settings can be found at:

- Account & Settings page: see Chapter LinkedIn Functionality

- Home Page: see Chapter LinkedIn Functionality

- Settings page of a Group: Select a Group and then the tab "Settings"

Send invitations from Outlook

Most people use the LinkedIn website to send invitations to other people. This is also possible from within Outlook.

To be able to do that you have to download the free Outlook Toolbar which can be found at the bottom of every page under "Tools".

Once you have installed the Outlook Toolbar, in every email you see a small "Info" icon on the right hand side.

When you move your mouse over the icon, you have the possibility to "invite" the person (if he is not in your network on LinkedIn yet) or "keep in touch" (you get a reminder if you haven't emailed with this person in 60 days).

LinkedIn helps to increase the ranking of your websites in search engines

Without making it too technical: websites get better rankings if they get links from popular websites. So what you need to do in your Profile is list one, two or three of your websites.

To increase the chances for a high ranking put the words you want to be found with, in the name of the description. How to do this? Choose "Other" and then give the website the name you want it to have. This doesn't have to be the official name of the website. So you can use keywords you want to be found with. Always make sure that it is still readable.

Apply this same tactic on all the other online business and social networks you are a member of.

Everybody in the chain can read every message of an introduction

When you send an introduction request to someone via "Get introduced through a connection", you always have to write two messages: one for the final recipient and one for your first degree contact.

Be aware that everybody who is "in the chain" can read all messages. In practice this means that your first degree contact can read your message to him and the final recipient, that the second degree contact can read your two messages and the message from your first degree contact to him and that the final recipient can read your two messages, the message from your first degree contact to your second degree contact and from the second degree contact to him.

So always be professional in the messages you send whether it is an introduction request from yourself or whether you forward a message from someone else.

I think it was Warren Buffet who said, "It takes a lifetime to build a reputation, but only a few seconds to destroy it."

Name is automatically included when sending invitations to imported contacts

When you have imported contacts from Outlook, Webmail or another email program, you can select people to send an invitation message to connect with you.

As I already mentioned before, make sure this message is (semi-) personal. A good way to make a message personal is to use the other person's name. The good news is that LinkedIn does that for you. The bad news is that you can't see it (there is no preview for this message) and you can't change what LinkedIn puts there.

So what does LinkedIn put there? The first name. Nothing more, nothing less. So not "HI John" or "John Smith" but "John".

Now you know this, use this information wisely!

Groups can help you raise your visibility

In the first chapter I explained the Golden Triangle of networking: sharing/ giving, asking and thanking. By taking actions on those three levels you will strengthen your relationships with your network.

Groups are an excellent place to build relationships and increase your visibility and credibility at the same time. How?

- **Giving/Sharing**: answer questions in the Discussion forums and post RELEVANT articles in the News section.

- **Asking**: ask for help and information. Always make sure you have given thought to your question. Then people will gladly help you and take the opportunity to build a relationship with you and the other members.

- **Thanking**: thank someone in public, in a current Discussion or open a new one. Be specific and generous (but don't overdo it).

Amount of Groups you can join is limited

Not many people know that the amount of Groups they can join is limited to 50. In the beginning there was no limit, so some people had to leave some Groups when LinkedIn imposed this limit.

For some this can be annoying, but most of us will only join a couple of Groups. In my opinion it is better to be an active member in some of the Groups, than wanting to be a member of hundreds of Groups.

Groups have an initial limit of 1000 members

If you are joining a Group, but are not accepted immediately it could be that the Group has reached the limit of 1000 members. This is not a real problem, but the Group Manager needs to ask LinkedIn management to increase the number. This can take a day or two. So if your membership is not approved, check the number of members and when it is 1000 just be patient.

Abusing Answers might block you from being able to ask questions ever again

If you abuse Answers to promote your services or to post job offers, you might be blocked from using Answers ever again.

When you ask a question, people can flag this question.

This is how it works (from the LinkedIn Help pages):

Flagging in "Answers" allows you and other LinkedIn members to make sure the questions being asked (and answers given) are the most useful and valuable. Flagging helps set the standards by which Answers operates. If you believe the content of that question or an answer is inappropriate for LinkedIn Answers you may flag that question by using the "Flag question as..." or "Flag answer as" link just below the text. When you flag a question, you'll be able to select from a drop down of reasons. Some reason why you might flag an item could be:

- *It is an advertisement.*
- *It contains inappropriate content.*
- *It is a connection building spam.*
- *It is a duplicate of another question asked by this person.*
- *It is a job-seeking message.*

Members asking the question may flag and remove a comment at any time. Members flagging a question may need more than one flag to remove the question from public view. Users who ask many questions which are flagged may be blocked from asking further questions.

How to become an "expert"

The first step to possibly earn "expert points" is answering questions in the Answers section. The person who asked the question can then award the best answer with an "expert point". So it is not because you have answered a question that you are awarded "expert points". Only one person, the one with the best answer, gets a point.

Remark: you can't earn expert points when you answer a question in a private message or in a Discussion, only via Answers.

Where can I find the invitations and messages I have sent and received?

You might expect to find all the invitations and messages you have received in your Inbox. LinkedIn works a little bit different: when you have answered it is automatically moved to another folder. You can find them under "Inbox" in the left hand menu. Sometimes it is hard to remember if it was a message or an invitation you sent or received. In that case you might have to look in two places.

For messages: click "Messages". Standard the messages you have received are shown. At the top of the page (but in the same "frame") you see the word "Sent". Click on that word to retrieve the messages you have sent.

For invitations: click "Invitations". Standard the messages you have received are shown. At the top of the page (but in the same "frame") you see the word "Sent". Click on that word to retrieve the invitations you have sent.

What will happen when I remove a connection? Will he be notified?

There are occasions you want to remove some of your contacts. The reasons might be that something happened between you and another person, that you are changing jobs or that you are reorienting yourself and don't want to be associated with a certain industry anymore. Personally only the first reason would be reason enough for me to remove a connection. In the other cases you might never know who they know or who can help you in your new situation.

Before I show you how to remove a connection, let 's start with a question that many people have: "I don't want to be connected anymore to that person, but I don't want him to know that because I don't want to get in trouble with him."

The answer is: no, the person you remove as a connection won't be notified.

These are the steps to remove someone:

1. In the left menu, click "Contacts".

2. In the new page you will see at the top right hand side: "Remove Connections".

3. Choose the connections you want remove and click the button "Remove connections".

The connections will not be notified that they have been removed. They will be added to your list of "Imported Contacts" in case you want to re-invite them later.

Can I download the contact details of my connections?

Yes, you can. There are two ways:

1. Individuals: go to their Profile. On the top right hand side you see a few icons. The first one is a printer, the third one a card with a small green arrow. If you go over it with your mouse it says "Download V-Card". Click this icon. Click on "save" if you want to save this as a new contact card in your email program.

2. All your connections:

   a. Go to "Contacts" or "Connections" in the left hand menu (this will give you the same page).

   b. Scroll down to the bottom of this page. You will see "Export Connections". Click on the text.

   c. Choose the email program you are using and click on "Export".

d. Download the file (you might have to give permission in your browser to do this action).

e. Read the instructions on the page on LinkedIn about how to import the file.

Timesaving Tip: the only details you will get are First Name, Last Name, Email address, Company and Job Title. If you want more contact details without having to do anything more yourself, get the Plaxo toolbar for your email program (see in the chapter "Free Tools to save you time when working with LinkedIn"). If the other person is also a Plaxo member all his details are automatically filled in. Of course this only works when the other person is also a Plaxo member, so it won't work for all your contacts, but if you have many connections on LinkedIn, this can save hours of work!

What happens when I choose "I Don't Know This Person" when I receive an invitation?

When someone has received 5 times the response "I Don't Know This Person" his possibilities to link with other people are very limited. He can only invite people whose email address he knows.

This is LinkedIn's way to limit spamming.

Most of the times I can't see the name of the person "Who viewed my profile"

Some people would like to know who visited their Profile. They then see most of the times only descriptions and not names. Some of them then pay for an upgraded account. However, that won't help. Paying won't get you this information.

How does it work then? Everybody has the choice which information you see when he visits your Profile. This is part of the privacy policy of LinkedIn.

Where can you find this?

• Go to "Account & Settings"

- Under "Privacy Settings" go to "Profile Views"

- Then there are three options under "What will be shown to other LinkedIn users when you view their profiles?"

  o Show my name and headline

  o Only show my anonymous Profile characteristics, such as industry and title (Default)

  o Don't show users that I've viewed their Profile

Since the second option is the default one and almost nobody changes the default settings, you will almost never see the name of the person who visited your Profile.

How did I get two (or more) accounts on LinkedIn?

Sometimes people find themselves having two or more accounts without understanding how this happened. Most of the times it is one of these two scenarios:

1. At a certain point in time they got an invitation from someone on their home email address, responded to it and made a Profile. Then forgot about it. Then after a year their colleagues were talking about it and they decided to make a LinkedIn Profile using their work email address.

2. They made a Profile on LinkedIn using their work address and got some connections. After a few weeks someone sends them an invitation via their home email address. They accept it and without realizing it they are making a new Profile.

So the reason for multiple accounts are different email accounts. Email addresses are used as the unique identifier.

To prevent this, you can list all your email addresses in one Profile.

When you already have more than one Profile, LinkedIn suggests you pick one, reinvite the people from the other account(s), and then go to "Account & Settings" and "Close your Account" using as reason "I have a duplicate account".

What happens with my contacts when I import them? Can everybody see them?

No. Only you can see them.

LinkedIn is also a licensee of the TRUSTe Privacy Program. In its Privacy Policy, LinkedIn declares it adherence to the following key privacy principles:

- LinkedIn will never rent or sell your personally identifiable information to third parties for marketing purposes.

- LinkedIn will never share your contact information with another user without your consent.

- Any sensitive information you provide will be secured with all industry standard protocols and technology.

How can I add my event to the Events list?

At the moment of writing this book the Event functionality was pretty new. I expect LinkedIn to expand this functionality in the future.

To add an event:

- Go to "Applications" on the left hand menu.
- Click on the + sign.
- Click on "Events".
- At the top of the new page, click on "Add Event"

How do I change who can contact me?

Some people choose to only receive invitations from people they know or get introductions via their network. LinkedIn helps you to decide who you want to get invitations and messages from.

How to change these settings?

- Go to "Account & Settings" (top of the page)
- Then look for "Email notifications"
  - o Click on "Contact Settings"

- What type of messages will you accept?

  » **I'll accept Introductions and InMail** (default): InMail means that people who have an upgraded account can contact you even if you don't know them.

  » **I'll accept only Introductions**: people you don't know can only reach you via your first degree contacts.

- The settings on the rest of the page are to give people more information about what you are interested in. It doesn't influence who can contact you.

  o Click on "Invitation Filtering"

  - **All invitations (Recommended):** Default.

  - **Only invitations from people who know my email address or appear in my "Imported Contacts" list**: if you get too many unwanted invitations you can choose this option. However, if your email address is easy to construct, some people will still use it.

  - **Only invitations from people who appear in my "Imported Contacts" list**: if you choose this option, make sure you have imported all the people from your email program.

Playing with the combination of these settings will help you to receive the invitations and introductions you want and filter out the rest.

Why are some posts in Discussions higher than others?

Normally the Discussions are ranked by date. The most recent post or comment is on top.

However, Group Managers have the ability to make some posts "featured" (you see this mentioned on top of the title of the post). These featured posts will be shown first and then the most recent posts/comments.

Why does LinkedIn work with a (confusing) area designation instead of the town my company is situated?

I have received this question especially from many people in Belgium. This is a small, but complex country, which is divided in a Dutch and a French speaking part. Through the area code of LinkedIn some companies who are situated in the Dutch speaking part now seem to be located in the French speaking part (and vice versa). This can be very confusing, especially when potential customers who look for a supplier, which is situated in the same "language area", use this area code.

For the moment it doesn't look like LinkedIn is going to change anything about that. The reason they use the area code is for safety and privacy reasons.

Tip: if you are not happy with the area designation, change the location to another city. However, don't choose one too far away from your current location, because it might influence your search results if you use the location parameter in your advanced searches.

Conclusion of this chapter

In this chapter you have received some insights in the behavior of LinkedIn. Think about this advice when using LinkedIn. Also come back to this chapter when you have a question yourself.

If you haven't found an answer to your question, look in the Help section of LinkedIn. That's also the place where I go when I have a question. You also might consult the "Answers" section on LinkedIn (subcategory Using LinkedIn). If you haven't found an answer yet, you can always contact the LinkedIn Help Desk (also via the "Help" function).

The latest updates can be found on the LinkedIn blog:
http://blog.linkedin.com

Since LinkedIn is a tool and not a goal you want to get the most out of it while spending as little time on it as possible. I don't mean to automate your responses and messages to people, but to use tools that help you to do things faster. And the good news is: there are many free tools! You'll find them in the next chapter.

Free Tools To Save You Time When Working With LinkedIn

Many people don't want to work with LinkedIn or another online network because they don't have time to do it.

I hope that you understand by now the tremendous value of LinkedIn. And also that it doesn't take that much of your time. Of course there are the initial steps to build your network. But afterwards you can reap the rewards by finding the right people very fast.

However, when you receive many messages and are building a huge network, some extra tools that can help you do more in less time are more than welcome.

In this chapter I will show you some of the tools that LinkedIn offers and also some other tools that will make your online networking life much easier. All tools mentioned in this chapter are free.

LinkedIn Tools

LinkedIn Outlook Toolbar

Download the free Outlook Toolbar, which can be found at the bottom of every page under "Tools".

Once you have installed the Outlook Toolbar, you get these extra features in Outlook:

- **Dashboard Button**: overview of actions

- **Grab Button**: when you select the email signature of someone and then click on the "Grab" button a new contact card is automatically created with the details of the signature automatically filled in. Some remarks for this function:

    o Street, town, state and country data are not always retrieved. For the other contact details this works almost always perfect!

    o Can be used from within the preview pane and from within an opened email.

    o To change the folder where the new contact cards are saved: click "Dashboard", "Preferences" and then "General".

- **Search bar**: search in LinkedIn from within Outlook. The LinkedIn website will then show the results in Outlook.

- **"Info" icon in emails**: when you move your mouse over the icon, you have the possibility to "invite" the person (if he is not in your network on LinkedIn yet) or "keep in touch" (you get a reminder if you haven't emailed with this person in 60 days).

LinkedIn Browser Toolbar

Download the free Internet Explorer or Firefox Toolbar, which can be found at the bottom of every page under "Tools".

After installing the Toolbar these are the tools that are available in the browser:

- **Search bar**: search in LinkedIn from the toolbar (so you don't have to go to the website).

- **Bookmarks**: after you have bookmarked some Profiles on LinkedIn, you can manage them from here.

- **JobInsider**: opens up a new pane in your browser. When looking at job postings in your normal browser window you can use this extra pane to look up how you are connected to people from the organization you are interested in.

Widgets

LinkedIn Widgets are small applications that other organizations can use on their website or blog. They can be found at the bottom of every page under "Tools / Developers". At the time of writing there were not many widgets, but it seems that LinkedIn wants to offer more in the future. These are the currently available widgets:

Company Insider

Description from the LinkedIn website: *"Let your users discover how they are connected to companies on your site. You pass a company name and we'll show how many people the user knows and a few sample names. This widget works great for news sites and blogs, letting readers connect to people at companies you mention. It also works well on jobs sites where job seekers can see who they know at hiring companies. Use it anywhere to inject professional networking into your site."*

Sounds interesting, but maybe more for portal websites than for most organizations.

Share on LinkedIn

Description from the LinkedIn website: *"Add a Share on LinkedIn link to your website or blog allowing your users to share your content with their LinkedIn connections or networks. This gives your content legs: one user visits your site and can notify literally tens, hundreds, or thousands of others. Works great for news sites, blogs, and other content–rich sites.*

For visibility reasons it might be a good tool. If you put this widget on your blog or your own website and your LinkedIn connections use it, you might get some extra visibility.

Tools to Make Life on LinkedIn Easier

Next to the tools LinkedIn offers itself, there are also some other tools that can help you save time or increase your results on LinkedIn.

Texter

This is a small tool that allows you to replace chunks of text with what they call a "hotstring". What does this mean in practice?

Do you remember the tip about how to deal with invitations from people you don't know? This was the text that I use myself:

> *HI xxx,*
>
> *Thank you for your invitation to connect!*
>
> *Unfortunately I meet so many people that I can't always "put the name and face together".*
>
> *Can you help me by reminding me where we met?*
>
> *Thanks and ... have a great networking day!*
>
> *Jan*

I don't like repeating work and it also takes some time to write this message. So I used Texter to create a "hotstring" called link-inv. When I type "link-inv" and then hit "enter" the text above appears. The only thing I still need to do is replace xxx with the actual name of the person who invited me.

Of course you can also use these hotstrings for many other chunks of text you use frequently in your daily job.

You can download Texter for free from the Lifehacker website: http://lifehacker.com/software/texter/lifehacker-code-texter-windows-238306.php

Thanks go to lifehacker, Bert Verdonck (www.bertverdonck.com) for sharing this one.

Google Alerts

Google Alerts give you updates on specific topics or people whenever something on the web is published about them.

Setup of this free tool is very easy:

- Go to www.google.com/alerts
- Then set the parameters:

  - Search term: topic or person you want to get information about
  - Type: where you want Google Alerts to search for you (Blogs, Videos, Web,...)
  - How often: as-it-happens, once a day or once a week
  - Email address: you receive the alert via email

When would you use this? To follow the news on a prospect or a company you want to work for. Or for updates on an expert, information for your project or for trends in the marketplace.

This allows you to share information with your network when you are maintaining your contacts. It also gives you something to talk or write about when you contact someone.

Google Keyword Tool

LinkedIn is a great tool to give you more visibility and build the brand of the organization you work for or your personal brand.

To increase your chances to be found on LinkedIn and also on the web, you need to use the right words. Many times we are "blinded" by the jargon we use in our own company or industry. Someone who is looking for our expertise might never use these words.

To help you with that there is the Google Keyword Tool. It is primarily used to find synonyms and alternatives for ads on Google, but you can use it to find the right words for your Profile too!

This free tool can be found at: https://adwords.google.com/select/KeywordToolExternal (or search on "Google Keyword Tool").

One remark: don't overdo it. Don't stuff your Profile with keywords. People still need to be able to read it.

Tools That Make your Virtual Networking Life Easier

Much of our virtual networking life goes via email. Here are a few tools that can help you spend less time and be more effective.

Plaxo Toolbar

Plaxo is nowadays more known for its online networking platform Plaxo Pulse (see the appendix about other networking websites). The free Plaxo toolbar gives you some extra tools in your email program (Outlook, Outlook Express, Mac, Mozilla Thunderbird). I want to share the most interesting ones with you:

- **Automatic fill of contact details in a contact card**: when you open a new contact card and only fill in the email address then Plaxo will search whether or not this person is also a Plaxo member. If so, the contact details of this person that he has filled in on his Plaxo profile, are automatically filled in on the contact card. So you don't have to type in all the contact details from people anymore. This is useful when you have downloaded someone's contact details from LinkedIn. Or when you have met someone in person and you have exchanged business cards.

- **Automatic updates of changes**: if someone changes his contact details on Plaxo, this is automatically updated in all the address books that are connected with this person.

- **Build Address Book**: find all the people you have exchanged emails with, but who are not in your contact folder yet. This tool will search emails for email addresses which are not in your contact folder yet. You can then make contact cards for these people. If they are also a Plaxo member their contact details are automatically filled in.

- **Ask for updates**: you can ask the people in your address book to check whether the information you have in your address book about them is still up to date. You can also use this in the last step of the "Build Address Book" process. Remember to change the standard message with a (semi) personal one!

- Remark:

  - Plaxo works with email address as identifier. However, you can have multiple email addresses for one profile. So it is always good to have a personal email address and a professional one linked to your profile. If you change jobs, you can still use your account and every Plaxo member you are connected with is automatically updated.

You can download the free Plaxo toolbar from the website www.plaxo.com Scroll to the bottom of the page and click on "Downloads".

Xobni

Another tool that can boost your efficiency communicating with people is Xobni. This free tool is only available for Outlook at the moment of writing.

Xobnl (the reverse of Inbox) puts another "layer" on emails. Outlook is email centric, while Xobnl is people centric.

What does this mean?

After installing Xobnl you get an extra toolbar next to your emails. In this toolbar you will find information about the sender of the email:

- **Contact details**: derived from signatures in emails and from LinkedIn if this person has a Profile on LinkedIn.
- **Network**: the people who were in "to" or "cc" in the emails you have exchanged with this person. Although it is not certain that they actually know each other, there is a chance they do.
- **Conversations**: emails you have exchanged with each other independent of the folder you have stored them in.
- **Files Exchanged**: files in attachment of the emails you have exchanged with each other independent of the folder you have stored them in.
- **Emails exchanged**: you see a visual chart of the times you sent emails to this person and when he sent you emails. You can use this information to see when is the best time to call someone (= when he sends most of the emails because then he is at his desk).
- **Schedule time with**: when you click on this link Xobnl looks up in your Outlook calendar when you have free moments in the coming period and puts them together in an email you can send to the other person.

It is clear that this tool gives you another view on your emails and makes it easier to contact someone and to retrieve the emails and files you have exchanged with each other. Since Xobni is email address based, you still have to be careful to rely on the emails and files presented if the other person uses more than one email address to communicate with you.

HelloTxt

If you use the "Status Update" feature not only on LinkedIn, but also on other platforms like Plaxo, Facebook, Twitter and MySpace, you can save time by using a tool, which updates all these platforms for you.

One of the websites, which offers this free service, is: http://hellotxt.com

Thanks go to Joel Elad who mentioned this tool in "LinkedIn for Dummies".

TinyURL

Posting the URL of a website where people can find interesting information (for example, in Discussions, Answers or Status Updates on LinkedIn or on your own website or any other place) can be hard sometimes when it is a very long URL.

The link can break and most of the times it negatively affects the readability of a posting.

On the website TinyURL (http://tinyurl.com/) you can transform a long URL into a short one. This is a free service.

More tools that can help you to be more effective in your networking and referral strategy can be found on the Networking Coach website: www. networking-coach.com. We add interesting tools on a regular basis so stop by once in a while or follow the updates on the blog (www.janvermeiren.com)

Also check out these websites and blogs for more tools to make your (networking) life easier:

- www.lifehacker.com
- www.lifehacking.nl
- www.martijnaslander.nl
- http://blog.bertverdonck.com

Now you have some tools that will help you. Do you have to use them? No, you don't have to do anything, but know that the tools that are mentioned in this chapter are free and can help save you lots of time.

Epilogue

Now you know why you are (or should be) on LinkedIn, what it is (and what it is not) and how to use it to reach your goals faster than ever before.

However, knowledge alone is not enough. It's up to you to take action.

Remember that most people only start to build their network when it is too late: they start building it when they need it. Other people feel this "need", they sense the urgency, even online. And that repels them rather than it attracts them.

So start building your network now. If you do it following the 5 fundamental principles of networking and using the strategy in this book, results are guaranteed!

LinkedIn is not the only website. There are more online business networks. Many more. I selected a handful of them, which might be useful for you to use next to LinkedIn. Despite the fact that the features might be different, the fundamental principles and the "start with your goal in mind" apply to all of them. You find them in the appendix.

As I already mentioned: a book about a website is always dangerous: it can be outdated the minute it is published. But for me it is important you get the most value out of this book and out of LinkedIn. That's why I will publish updated parts of the book and extra tips whenever something changes or whenever I get new insights.

To get these updates and a free LinkedIn Profile Self Assessment, register at www.how-to-really-use-linkedin.com/updates.html. If you want to get even more out of your LinkedIn membership look at "Bought the book? Get even more out of LinkedIn" on www.how-to-really-use-linkedin.com.

To help you get even more value out of this book and to get even bigger results we have started the "Global Networking Group" on LinkedIn (http://www.linkedin.com/groups?home=&gid=1393777). It is open to anyone who wants to play by the rules of this Group. So come and join us and experience the power of networking via LinkedIn!

To your success!

Jan

PS: when you have closed your 100 million deal by applying the tips in this book or found your dream job, don't send me a check. Just write a Recommendation on LinkedIn with how the tips worked for you and you will make me happy as well ☺

Appendix: Other Online Business Networks

Of course LinkedIn is not the only online business network. However, at the time of writing it had the largest number of members. And also the lowest threshold to become a member. As a result many people from all over the world, from different industries and with different functions are now on LinkedIn. That is why the focus of this book is on LinkedIn.

However, there are many, many more online business networks and social networks. LinkedIn has its origins in the USA like many others, but also in Europe and Asia there are very popular online business networks. An De Jonghe has made a list of most of them in her book, "Social Networks Around the World". I will only list a few of them in this chapter. If you want to find more online social and business networks in your region, buy An's book.

Remark: since the online world changes so quickly the numbers of users will already have changed when you read this. Also some websites might have added some extra functions, which would cause a different review from my part.

Ecademy

URL	www.ecademy.com
Description	Ecademy is a social BUSINESS community. This means the emphasis is on the business part. However, there is also room for the more personal side so members can meet each other as "whole human beings". It is the most social business network for the moment. Central for the user experience on the website are the public and private clubs where members can give and receive help to each other. In many regions the added value of membership is in the network meetings and events the local representatives organize. Members report that this combination between online and offline networking makes the difference for them.
Number of users	300,000
Target Audience	Especially small business owners and freelancers.

Regional focus	World
Type of memberships	Free basic membership PowerNetworker (monthly fee) Blackstar (life membership)
Country of origin	United Kingdom
Remarks	• Feature rich, which makes long-term members happy, but is sometimes overwhelming for new users. • The combination of online and offline networking is a big plus!

Xing

URL	www.xing.com
Description	Xing is primarily a business network. Members can also list personal interests. Central for the user experience on the website are the forums where members can give and receive help to each other. In many regions the added value of membership is in the network meetings and events the local representatives organize. Members report that this combination between online and offline networking makes the difference for them.
Number of users	6.5 Million
Target Audience	Any professional
Regional focus	World
Type of memberships	Free basic membership Premium membership (monthly fee)

Country of origin	Germany
Remarks	<ul><li>Multilingual user interface lowers the threshold to participate in this network for people who don't speak English that well. For some people the downside of this is that they can't participate in discussions on forums when they don't speak the native language of the founder of that club.</li><li>The combination of online and offline networking is a big plus!</li></ul>

Viadeo

URL	www.viadeo.com
Description	Viadeo is primarily a business network. Members can also list personal interests. Central for the user experience on the website are the forums where members can give and receive help to each other. In many regions the added value of membership is in the network meetings and events the local representatives organize. Members report that this combination between online and offline networking makes the difference for them.
Number of users	4 Million
Target Audience	Any professional
Regional focus	World
Type of memberships	Free basic membership Premium membership (monthly fee)
Country of origin	France

Remarks	• Multilingual user interface lowers the threshold to participate in this network for people who don't speak English that well. For some people the downside of this is that they can't participate in discussions on forums when they don't speak the native language of the founder of that club.
	• The combination of online and offline networking is a big plus!
	• Half of the members are located in China.

Plaxo Pulse

URL	www.plaxo.com
Description	Plaxo Pulse is at the moment of writing still in beta version. According to the website Plaxo Pulse it is different from social and business networks because it wants to be a platform where other tools are brought together so people can share more with each other and keep up-to-date what they are doing.
	Many people already have an account on this platform since they were already a user of the Plaxo toolbar.
Number of users	20 Million
Target Audience	Any professional
Regional focus	World
Type of memberships	Free basic membership
	Premium membership (monthly fee)
Country of origin	USA

Remarks	• My opinion: at the moment of writing no real added value yet as a social or business network platform if you are also using other websites like LinkedIn.
	• The Plaxo toolbar for your email program is a very useful tool.
	• Huge potential because of the large user base.

Facebook

URL	www.facebook.com
Description	Facebook is a SOCIAL (business) network. Originated as a platform for college students to share personal interests, Facebook has grown exponentially. More and more professionals have an account on this website and also more and more organizations have virtual clubs.
	Central for the user experience on the website are the interactions between members (not only one-to-one as on the other websites, but also the ability to watch the interactions between friends) and the groups where members can give and receive help to each other.
Number of users	150 Million
Target Audience	Anyone
Regional focus	World
Type of memberships	Free membership
Country of origin	USA

Remarks	• The third party applications give Facebook an extra appeal and is probably the reason for its exponential growth. On the other hand this might also become the reason why people won't use it anymore because they get too many invitations for time consuming games and quizzes. • Has huge potential for professional interactions.

Ning

URL	www.ning.com
Description	Ning is a platform where people can create their own virtual community. Other than the other networking platforms where the user is central, here the community is central. Central for the user experience on the website are the communities where members can give and receive help to each other.
Number of users	250,000 networks (not users)
Target Audience	Anyone
Regional focus	World
Type of memberships	Free membership
Country of origin	USA
Remarks	• Limited profile information "forces" people to also have memberships on other sites. • Easy to create your own community.

Netwerklounge

URL	www.netwerklounge.be
Description	Netwerklounge is the virtual community of the Belgian organization Business Netwerk Cafe. Although it is a rather small community I still want to mention it because many readers of this book will be from my home country Belgium. Central for the user experience on the website are the interactions between members before and after the physical events and the forums where members can give and receive help to each other.
Number of users	5500
Target Audience	Any professional
Regional focus	Belgium
Type of memberships	Free membership
Country of origin	Belgium
Remarks	Primarily facilitates keeping in touch with the other participants of the events of Business Netwerk Cafe, but is also open to other people.

About the author Jan Vermeiren

Jan Vermeiren is thé expert in Belgium, the Netherlands and the rest of Europe when it comes to networking and referrals. He is the founder of Networking Coach and according to HR Tribune one of Belgians top10 speakers.

Jan and his team not only provide (key note) presentations, training courses and personal coaching about networking and referrals, but also advise organizations how to stimulate networking at their own events and how to integrate networking in their sales and recruitment strategy.

Besides that he is also regularly interviewed about networking and referrals by different media like Belgian national television and radio (De Zevende Dag, Lichtpunt, Radio 1), newspapers and websites (Forbes), job sites (Vacature.com, Jobat) and the magazines of several Chambers of Commerce.

Jan is the author of the networking book, "Let's Connect!," the networking CD "Let's Connect at an Event!," the "Everlasting Referrals Home Study Course" and now also of "How to REALLY use LinkedIn".

The US version of Let's Connect reached the Amazon bestseller list on October 9, 2007 with a number 2 position in marketing books and number 9 in management books. This made Jan the first Belgian author to reach this position.

Jan and his team are hired by large international companies like Alcatel, Deloitte, DuPont, IBM, ING, Mobistar, Nike, SAP and Sun Microsystems as well as by small companies and freelancers.

Jan is also a guest lecturer in the international MBA programs of Vlerick Leuven Gent Management School (Belgium) and RSM Erasmus University Rotterdam (the Netherlands).

Other books and websites

From the same author

- Vermeiren Jan, Let's Connect!
- Vermeiren Jan, Let's Connect at an Event (CD)
- Vermeiren Jan, Everlasting Referrals Home Study Course

Books that are mentioned in this book

- Alba Jason, I'm on LinkedIn, now what?
- Allen Scott and Teten David, The Virtual Handshake
- Baker Wayne, Networking Smart
- Burg Bob, Endless Referrals
- Burg Bob, The Go Giver
- Butow Eric and Taylor Kathleen, How to Succeed in Business using LinkedIn
- Comaford-Lynch Christine, Rules for Renegades
- Covey Stephen MR, The Speed of Trust
- De Jonghe An, Social Networks Around The World
- Elad Joel, LinkedIn for Dummies
- Fisher Donna, People Power
- Valkenburg Jacco, Recruitment via LinkedIn

Some websites, which group super connectors or give additional information about LinkedIn

- TopLinkedIn: http://www.toplinkedin.com
- TopLinkedIn Discussion Group: http://finance.groups.yahoo.com/group/TOPLINKEDIN
- LIONS: http://finance.groups.yahoo.com/group/linkedinlions
- MLPF: http://www.mylinkedinpowerforum.com
- MyLink500: http://mylink500.com
- MyLinkWiki: http://toplinkedin.pbwiki.com
- LinkedIntelligence: http://www.linkedintelligence.com
- MyLinkSearch: http://www.mylinksearch.com

Other Products and Services of Networking Coach

Other than other training companies Jan Vermeiren and the team of Networking Coach are specialized in the topics of online and offline networking and referrals. We don't do anything else (but are happy to connect you with a specialist from our network).

Products

- **Free networking e-course:** www.networking-coach.com

- **Network book and bestseller, "Let's Connect!** A practical guide for networking at events and on the web for every professional whether in sales or not"
  (free light version available at www.letsconnect.be)

- **Network CD "Let's Connect at an Event**, 30 immediately applicable networking tips to make every event a success"
  (free light version available at www.networking-coach.com)

- **Everlasting Referrals Home Study Course:** how to create a network of ambassadors that will bring in customer after customer so you don't ever have to cold call again
  (www.everlasting-referrals.com)

- **How to REALLY use LinkedIn** (yes, this book ☺)

Services

For individuals:

- **Workshops and training courses** (open format and tailored in-company versions):

  - Introduction session networking or referrals (half day)

  - What's Your Sticky Story©? (half day)

  - Proactive Networker Training Course (2 days)

  - Everlasting Referrals Training Course (2 days, for business owners and sales people)

  - Power of Networking and Referrals Course (3 days, for business owners and sales people)

- o   Smart Networking Training Course (3,5 days)
- o   We happily provide tailored training courses in class room format, via teleseminars or webinars or a combination of these formats

- **(Interactive) Presentations and Key Note Speeches,** some examples:

  - o   "Everlasting Referrals, No More Cold Calls". What are the 7 main reasons that most organizations don't get (spontaneous) referrals and what to do about it?
  - o   "Your Net Works". How to tap into the Power of your Network.
  - o   "What's your Sticky Story©?" How to answer "And what do you do?" in a way you will be remembered.
  - o   "Help, I need a new job": How to tap into the power of your network to find a new job.
  - o   "Oh no, another reception". How to network more efficiently, more effectively and with more fun at a business drink, conference or any other event.
  - o   "How to REALLY use LinkedIn". How to find and get introduced to the people who can help you reach your goals using LinkedIn (can be adapted to find new customers, a new job, new employees, suppliers, partners or experts)."

All interactive presentations, keynote speeches and training courses are adapted to the audience and the situation of the organization.

Detailed descriptions and the calendar of open training courses and seminars can be found at www.networking-coach.com

For organizations:

- Interactive presentations and key note speeches (see above)
- Strategic consulting about how to integrate networking and referrals in the sales strategy
- Strategic consulting about how to integrate networking and referrals in the recruitment strategy
- Advice on how to stimulate networking between the participants of a networking event

References:

These are some of the **companies and professional organizations** the team of Networking Coach has worked for:

Accenture, Agoria, Alcatel, Antwerp Diamond Bank, Belgacom, BIASS, Bosch, Colruyt, CTG, Deloitte, Delta Lloyd Bank, Dexia, Dupont, Eandis, ECM Congres (European Cities Marketing), EDS, Ernst & Young, Euphony, Fortis, Gemeente Den Haag, Getronics, IBM, ING, Janssen Farmaceutica, Johnson Controls, KBC, Leaseplan, Mobistar, MOVI, Nationale Bank van België, Nike, Partena, Resources Global Professionals, SAP, SD Worx, Securex, Siemens, SOFIA, Stad Gent, Stichting Kwaliteitskring Limburg, Stichting Marketing, Sun Microsystems, Telenet, TNT, TvZ-congres, Unisys, Unizo, USG People, Van Breda Risks & Benefits, VIK, VKW, Vlaamse Overheid Bestuurszaken, VMA, VOKA, VVSG, Women and Network and many small business owners and freelancers.

These are some of the **universities, alumnI organizations and non-profit organizations** the Networking Coach team has worked for:

Aiesec, Ehsal Alumni, RSM Erasmus International MBA Rotterdam, Hogeschool Arnhem Nijmegen Alumni, JCI (Junior Chamber International), Karel De Grote Hogeschool, Markant, Palliatieve Zorgen Netwerk, Provinciale Hogeschool Limburg, PSA Holland (Professional Speakers Association Holland), Solvay Business School Alumni, University of Antwerp Management School and Vlerick Leuven Management School International MBA.

Subscribe also to the monthly e-newsletter with tips from Jan Vermeiren and his fellow network and referral experts from all over the world (www.networking-coach.com).

Read Jan's weekly blog full of networking and referral tips at www.janvermeiren.com

Get even more out of this book

As I already mentioned: a book about a website is always dangerous: it can be outdated the minute it is published. But to me it is important you get the most value out of this book and out of LinkedIn. That's why I will publish **updated parts of the book** and extra tips whenever something changes or whenever I get new insights.

To get this for free plus a **free LinkedIn Profile Assessment**, sign up for them at www.how-to-really-use-linkedin.com/updates.html. You will also get free access to some other great resources to help you to leverage the power of your network to achieve your goals.

To help you get even more value out of this book and to get even bigger results we have started the "**Global Networking Group**" on LinkedIn (http://www.linkedin.com/groups?home=&gid=1393777). It is open to anyone who wants to play by the rules of this Group. So come and join us!

If you really want to get the most out of your LinkedIn membership, consider buying the **LinkedIn Power Package** or the **LinkedIn Personal Profiling Package**. These packages can be found at www.how-to-really-use-linkedin. com.

So what are you waiting for?
Go to www.how-to-really-use-linkedin.com/updates.html and experience the power of networking via LinkedIn!

Made in the USA